HEALTHCARE
STEWARDSHIP

A CALL TO ACTION FOR A 21ST CENTURY SUSTAINABLE
AMERICAN HEALTHCARE DELIVERY SYSTEM

DALE J. BLOCK
MD, MBA, DABFM

**Quantum
Discovery**
A LITERARY AGENCY

Library of Congress Control Number: 2024920383

ISBN
978-1-964982-69-4 (Paperback)
978-1-964982-70-0 (eBook)
978-1-964982-68-7 (Hardcover)

DEDICATION

I dedicate this book to my wife, Ellen; my three sons, Aaron, Jeremy, and Stuart; their respective spouses, John, Valerie, and Christina; and my grandchildren, Jude, Emilia, and Jax. I also dedicate this book to the memory of my daughter, Julie, whose influence has been a constant inspiration throughout my medical career, motivating me to continually strive to educate the next generation of healers.

TABLE OF CONTENTS

PREFACE

Primum non nocere

Primum non nocere, or *first, do no harm*, is a core ethical principle in healthcare that underscores the commitment to preventing harm in patient care. This principle helps guide healthcare professionals to carefully evaluate the potential risks and benefits of any intervention or treatment. By adhering to *primum non nocere*, clinicians ensure that their actions prioritize patient safety and minimize unnecessary safety risks. It promotes a careful, evidence-based approach to critical decision-making and logical reasoning, emphasizing the importance of avoiding interventions that could lead to adverse effects or complications. This principle fosters trust, truthfulness, and confidence between patients and providers, reinforcing the ethical foundation of medical practice.

Healthcare stewardship is defined as the responsible management of limited healthcare resources to ensure the most effective and ethical delivery of healthcare goods and services. It encompasses principles of efficiency, sustainability, and fairness, ensuring that the limited healthcare resources are used wisely and equitably to maximize patient benefit. *Primum non nocere* aligns closely with healthcare stewardship, as both principles focus on minimizing harm and optimizing outcomes with the appropriate use of limited resources. Stewardship, alone, involves not only managing physical resources but also considering the broader impact of healthcare decisions on patient safety, quality of care, and overall system efficiency. By integrating *primum non nocere* with effective stewardship principles and practices, healthcare providers can enhance the quality and safety of delivered care, lower the total cost of that delivered care, and overall, ensure the sustainability of evidence-based health services delivered in the US, ultimately leading to better patient outcomes and a more equitable healthcare system.

Healthcare Stewardship: A Call to Action for a 21st Century Sustainable American Healthcare Delivery System examines how major changes in the U.S. healthcare delivery system can reshape it into a sustainable, holistic, and integrated model of empirically-supported healthcare services and management for the 21st century. This book emphasizes foundational principles and practices of healthcare stewardship and capacity-building improvements, with *primum non nocere* serving as the guiding overarching principle of reason and humility. A major paradigm shift is essential to accomplish this urgent call to action for the essential changes needed to innovate and establish a successful and sustainable US healthcare delivery system.

Healthcare Stewardship is the first authoritative text on healthcare services and management to apply the principles and practices of stewardship—a concept with religious origins dating back to biblical times—to the production and delivery of limited healthcare goods and services. Practicing stewardship is really quite simple. Limited healthcare resources that are available for Americans must be used in a manner that is clinically, ethically, politically, environmentally and socially responsible. Regrettably, simplicity in the U.S. healthcare delivery system is an unachievable goal. Bureaucracies at the federal, state, and local levels have contributed to making it the most complex healthcare delivery system in the world. The purpose of this book on healthcare stewardship is to spark a sense of urgency—a burning platform—with a call to action for a significant paradigm shift, guiding the transformation of the U.S. healthcare delivery system into a sustainable model of care accessible to all Americans.

My purpose in writing *Healthcare Stewardship* is to raise awareness among everyone affected by the American healthcare delivery system. This book seeks to illuminate the critical issues, challenges, and opportunities within the U.S. healthcare delivery system framework, fostering a collective understanding and commitment to improvement and innovation. By engaging healthcare professionals, policymakers, patients, and the public-at-large, I aim to inspire a sense of responsibility and drive meaningful change toward a more efficient, equitable, and sustainable American healthcare delivery system for all.

Dale J. Block, MD, MBA, DABFM

CHAPTER 1

21ST CENTURY EXISTENTIAL THREATS

1.1 EXISTENTIAL THREATS TO THE AMERICAN HEALTHCARE DELIVERY SYSTEM IN THE 21ST CENTURY

The American healthcare delivery system faces several existential threats in the 21st century, with one of the most pressing being the rising cost of healthcare (Lopes et al., 2024). High-cost expenses are a significant barrier for many individuals, leading to a substantial number of Americans being uninsured or underinsured. This financial strain affects not only patients but also healthcare providers and institutions, which struggle to balance high operating costs with the need to deliver high-quality care. The unsustainable cost trajectory threatens to widen health disparities, reduce access to essential healthcare services, and undermine the overall stability of the US healthcare delivery system.

Another existential threat is the increasing burden of chronic diseases, which account for the majority of healthcare spending in the United States (Chan et al., 2020; Lai et al., 2021; Vodovotz et al., 2020). Conditions such as diabetes, heart disease, cancer, dementia, and obesity are becoming more prevalent due to lifestyle factors and an aging population. Managing these diseases requires long-term, coordinated, comprehensive and complex care requiring significant resources, putting a strain on an already overstretched American healthcare system. Without effective strategies to prevent and manage chronic illnesses, the system risks being overwhelmed, compromising care quality, safety, and accessibility.

The American healthcare workforce crisis is another critical issue facing the American healthcare delivery system (de Vries et al, 2023). There is a growing shortage of healthcare professionals, including doctors, nurses, and allied health workers, exacerbated by an aging workforce and high rates of burnout and job dissatisfaction. This shortage impacts the delivery of care, leading to longer wait times, reduced patient access, and increased pressure on existing staff, which can compromise patient safety and outcomes. Addressing workforce issues is essential to maintaining a robust, responsive, and resilient American healthcare system capable of meeting current and future demands.

Additionally, the integration of technology and data privacy and security presents a significant challenge (Li et al., 2021; Okafor et al., 2023). While advancements in digital health technologies, such as electronic health records (EHRs) and telemedicine, have the potential to improve care delivery, they also introduce vulnerabilities related to data privacy and cybersecurity. The increasing frequency, magnitude, and sophistication of cyberattacks on healthcare systems pose a threat to patient information and overall system integrity. Ensuring robust cybersecurity measures and protecting patient data are critical to maintaining trust in the American healthcare system and safeguarding against disruptions that could impede care delivery.

Political and regulatory instability poses a continuous threat to the American healthcare delivery system (Thomas et al, 2020; Berman et al., 2022). Frequent changes in healthcare policy, funding, and regulations create an environment of uncertainty for providers, insurers, and patients. The politicization of healthcare issues can lead to abrupt policy shifts that disrupt the stability and predictability needed for effective long-term planning and investment in healthcare infrastructure. Ensuring a stable and supportive regulatory environment is crucial for fostering innovation, improving care delivery, and addressing the complex challenges facing the healthcare system in the 21st century.

Racism remains a profound existential threat to American society, manifesting not only in social and economic disparities but also deeply impacting the healthcare delivery system (Yearby et al., 2022, Feagin et al., 2014). Systemic racism results in unequal access to healthcare, poorer health outcomes, and higher mortality rates for marginalized communities, particularly African Americans, Hispanics, and Native Americans. Discrimination and bias within the healthcare system has led to mistrust among minority populations, deterring them from seeking necessary medical care. This mistrust is compounded by historical injustices and ongoing disparities in treatment and diagnosis. Addressing racism in healthcare requires comprehensive policy changes, cultural competency training for healthcare providers, and a commitment to equity and justice to ensure that all individuals receive fair and adequate medical attention.

Natural disasters pose a significant threat to the American healthcare delivery system by overwhelming medical infrastructure, disrupting supply chains, and displacing populations (Ferguson et al., 2024). Hurricanes, wildfires, earthquakes, and floods can destroy hospitals and clinics, leading to a sudden loss of critical healthcare services. In the aftermath of such disasters, there is often an increase in health emergencies, including injuries, infectious diseases, and mental health crises, which further strain the already stretched resources. Effective disaster preparedness and response plans, including robust infrastructure, efficient emergency services, and resilient healthcare systems, are essential to mitigate the impact of natural disasters on healthcare delivery. Additionally, ensuring that vulnerable populations have access to timely and effective medical care during and after disasters is crucial for minimizing health disparities.

Emerging infectious diseases, such as COVID-19, pose a grave threat to the American healthcare system by rapidly increasing the demand for medical services and exposing weaknesses in public health preparedness and response (Palagyi et al., 2019; Baker et al., 2022) These diseases can lead to widespread illness and death, placing immense pressure on hospitals, healthcare workers, and medical supplies. The COVID-19 pandemic highlighted the critical need for robust multi-level surveillance systems, rapid and coordinated response capabilities, and effective communication strategies to manage such crises. Additionally, it underscored the importance of global cooperation and investment in research and development for new evidence-based vaccines and treatments. Strengthening public health infrastructure, improving infection control practices, and ensuring equitable access to healthcare are vital to mitigate the impact of emerging infectious diseases on the healthcare system.

Economic inequality and inequity profoundly affect the American healthcare delivery system by creating barriers to access and perpetuating health disparities (Dickman et al., 2017; Horowitz et al., 2020). Individuals with lower socioeconomic status often lack adequate health insurance, face higher out-of-pocket costs, and experience difficulties in accessing quality care. These economic barriers result in delayed diagnoses, untreated conditions, and poorer overall health outcomes for disadvantaged populations. Furthermore, healthcare providers serving low-income communities may face financial constraints, limiting their ability to offer comprehensive services. Addressing economic inequality in healthcare requires policy interventions to expand insurance coverage, reduce costs, close health disparities, and invest in underserved areas. Ensuring that all individuals, regardless of their economic status, have access to high-quality healthcare is essential for promoting equity and improving public health outcomes.

Lastly, climate change significantly impacts the American healthcare delivery system by exacerbating health issues and increasing the frequency and severity of natural disasters (Ebi et al., 2021; Huggel et al., 2022; Seervai et al., 2022; Eckelman et al., 2020). Rising temperatures, air and water pollution, and extreme weather events contribute to a range of health problems, including respiratory diseases, heat-related illnesses, and vector-borne diseases. Vulnerable populations, such as the elderly, children, and those with chronic conditions, are particularly at risk. The healthcare system must adapt to these changes by enhancing resilience, improving emergency preparedness and response, and integrating climate considerations into multi-level public health planning. Additionally, addressing the root causes of climate change through sustainable practices and policies is crucial to mitigate its long-term effects on health and healthcare delivery. A proactive approach to climate change is necessary to protect public health and ensure the sustainability of healthcare systems in the face of environmental challenges.

1.2 A CALL TO ACTION: US HEALTHCARE DELIVERY MUST RESPOND TO EXISTENTIAL THREATS

The American healthcare delivery system faces an urgent call to action to address existential threats that challenge its capacity to provide integrated, holistic, comprehensive, effective, equitable, and sustainable care. Rising healthcare costs, workforce burn-out, informatics and cybersecurity, political and regulatory instability, institutional bias and racism, economic inequality and inequity, climate change and greenhouse gases emission, natural disasters and pandemics, and the rise of chronic diseases represent significant challenges that demand immediate and coordinated responses. To mitigate these threats, the American healthcare delivery system must prioritize resilience, innovation, and equity in its policies and practices (Witter et al., 2023; Biddle et al., 2020, Nzinga et al., 2021).

The US healthcare system must invest in building resilience against climate change (Lugten et al., 2022). This involves preparing for extreme weather events, such as hurricanes, wildfires, and heatwaves, which can disrupt healthcare services and exacerbate health conditions. Hospitals and healthcare facilities should adopt sustainable practices, such as reducing carbon footprints, improving energy efficiency, and using renewable energy sources. Additionally, healthcare providers need to integrate climate change considerations into public health planning and patient care, recognizing the impact of environmental factors on health outcomes and addressing them proactively.

The COVID-19 pandemic has highlighted the critical need for robust public health multi-level infrastructure, preparedness, and response (Metzl et al., 2020; Niles, 2023). Strengthening the healthcare delivery system's ability to respond to future pandemics requires enhanced surveillance, rapid response capabilities, and effective communication strategies. Investing in research and development for vaccines, therapeutics, and diagnostic tools is essential for staying ahead of emerging infectious diseases. Moreover, building a flexible and highly-trained healthcare workforce capable of scaling up in times of crisis, along with ensuring adequate supplies of personal protective equipment (PPE) and other essential resources, is crucial for maintaining healthcare services during pandemics.

Chronic diseases, such as diabetes, hypertension, heart disease, respiratory dysfunction, cancer, neurodegenerative disease and obesity, pose long-term existential threats to the healthcare system due to their prevalence and associated healthcare costs (Crawford et al., 2023). A shift towards proactive care and the promotion of healthy lifestyles and behaviors is essential in addressing these conditions. Healthcare providers should focus on early detection and evidence-based screening, patient education, health literacy, and community-based interventions led by community-based organizations that encourage healthy behaviors. Integrating technology, such as telehealth and remote patient monitoring, can enhance chronic disease management and reduce the burden on already stressed healthcare facilities. Policymakers and government regulators must also address the negative determinants of health, such as access to nutritious food, safe housing, and opportunities for physical activity, to prevent chronic diseases and improve population health.

An urgent call to action must focus on diversity, equity, and inclusion and must be at the forefront of the healthcare delivery system's response to existential threats of economic inequality and inequity, institutional bias and overt racism (Stanford, 2020). The disproportionate impact of these threats on marginalized communities underscores the need for equitable access to healthcare services. This requires addressing systemic barriers, such as racial and socioeconomic disparities and the discriminatory real estate practice of redlining, and ensuring that all individuals and the communities within which they live, work and play receive high quality healthcare services regardless of their background. Community engagement and partnerships with local organizations are vital in developing culturally appropriate interventions and reaching underserved populations. Additionally, data collection and analysis should focus on identifying and addressing health inequities to inform targeted strategies that promote health equity.

The American healthcare delivery system must act decisively to address the many existential threats described (Laprise, 2023). By adopting a proactive, integrated, comprehensive and holistic approach to providing a full range of healthcare services, the US healthcare delivery system can better protect the health, wellness, and well-being of individuals, families and communities creating a more sustainable and equitable future for all.

1.3 HEALTHCARE STEWARDSHIP: A FRAMEWORK FOR RESPONDING TO THE EXISTENTIAL THREATS

Introducing healthcare stewardship is a critical response to the urgent call to action for the American healthcare delivery system facing these existential threats (Brinkerhoff et al., 2019). Healthcare stewardship emphasizes responsible management of limited resources, proactive care, and long-term sustainability to ensure that healthcare systems are resilient, equitable, and effective. As the healthcare landscape grapples with challenges such as climate change, pandemics, and chronic diseases, the principles of stewardship offer a comprehensive framework for addressing these threats.

Healthcare stewardship involves the judicious use of limited healthcare resources to maximize health outcomes while minimizing waste and inefficiency. This requires a shift towards value-based care, where the focus is on patient outcomes rather than the volume of services provided. By prioritizing proactive care and early intervention, healthcare systems can reduce the burden of chronic diseases and prevent costly hospitalizations. Stewardship also means investing in sustainable practices, such as energy-efficient healthcare facilities, reducing carbon footprints, and promoting environmental health, to mitigate the impact of climate change on public health.

Proactive care is a cornerstone of healthcare stewardship. This involves anticipating and preparing for future health threats through robust public health infrastructure and emergency preparedness. For instance, the COVID-19 pandemic has underscored the need for rapid response capabilities, including the ability to quickly develop and distribute vaccines and therapeutics (Wong et al., 2022; NASEM, 2021). By fostering a culture of preparedness and continuous improvement, healthcare systems can better respond to pandemics and other emerging threats. Proactive care also includes integrating technology and data analytics to enhance disease surveillance, predict outbreaks, and tailor interventions to the specific needs of populations.

Equity is fundamental to healthcare stewardship. Ensuring that all individuals have access to high-quality care, regardless of their socioeconomic status, race, or geographic location, is essential for a resilient and fair healthcare system. This involves addressing social determinants of health and eliminating systemic barriers that contribute to health disparities. Healthcare stewards must advocate for policies that promote health equity and work collaboratively with community organizations to develop culturally appropriate and accessible healthcare services. By prioritizing equity, healthcare stewardship ensures that vulnerable populations are protected and that the benefits of healthcare innovations are shared broadly.

In conclusion, healthcare stewardship provides a strategic and ethical framework for responding to the existential threats facing the American healthcare delivery system. By emphasizing resource management, proactive care, and equity, stewardship ensures that healthcare systems are resilient, sustainable, and capable of delivering high-quality and cost-effective healthcare goods and services to all individuals in the right amount and at the right place. Embracing the principles of stewardship is crucial for addressing the complex and interconnected challenges of climate change, pandemics, and chronic diseases, ultimately leading to healthier and more equitable communities.

1.4 EXAMPLES OF HEALTHCARE STEWARDSHIP

Examples of healthcare stewardship span various aspects of healthcare delivery, policy-making, and resource management (Nasiri et al., 2019; Shams et al., 2021, Duplechan, 2022).

1. Resource Allocation

   a. Prioritizing Vaccinations: During flu seasons or pandemics, health authorities prioritize vaccination for high-risk groups, such as the elderly, healthcare workers, and individuals with chronic conditions. This ensures that limited vaccine supplies are used where they can have the greatest impact.

   b. Essential Medicines List: The World Health Organization (WHO) maintains a list of essential medicines that should be available to all healthcare systems. This helps countries prioritize their resources and ensure access to the most critical medications.

2. Evidence-Based Practice

   a. Clinical Guidelines: Developing and adhering to clinical practice guidelines for treating common conditions ensures that healthcare providers use the most effective and efficient treatment methods. This reduces variations in medical care and improves patient outcomes.

   b. Proactive Care Initiatives: Programs that promote preventive care, such as routine screenings for cancer or heart disease, help detect conditions early, reducing the need for more extensive and costly treatments later.

3. Health System Management

a. Integrated Care Models: Implementing integrated care models that coordinate services across primary, secondary, and tertiary care settings can reduce redundancies, improve patient outcomes, and lower healthcare costs.

b. Electronic Health Records (EHRs): Utilizing EHRs to streamline information sharing among healthcare providers can enhance care coordination, reduce medical errors, and improve the efficiency of healthcare delivery.

4. Environmental Stewardship

a. Sustainable Practices in Healthcare Facilities: Hospitals and clinics adopting environmentally sustainable practices, such as reducing waste, recycling medical materials, and using energy-efficient technologies, contribute to the overall sustainability of the healthcare system.

b. Green Procurement Policies: Healthcare organizations that prioritize the procurement of environmentally friendly products and services help reduce their ecological footprint and promote public health.

5. Ethical and Equitable Care

a. Community Health Programs: Initiatives that provide healthcare services to underserved and marginalized populations, such as mobile health clinics and community health worker programs, ensure that all individuals have access to necessary care.

b. Health Equity Policies: Developing and implementing policies that address social determinants of health, such as housing, education, and income, helps create a more equitable healthcare system.

6. Policy and Governance

a. Regulatory Oversight: Governments and health authorities provide regulatory oversight to ensure that healthcare providers adhere to standards of care, maintain patient safety, and use resources efficiently.

b. Public Health Campaigns: Campaigns to raise awareness about healthy lifestyles, vaccinations, and disease prevention are crucial in managing public health resources and preventing outbreaks of diseases.

These examples introduce and illustrate how healthcare stewardship involves an integrated and comprehensive approach to managing resources, improving care quality and safety, and ensuring equitable access to healthcare services.

1.5 REFERENCES

Baker, R. E., Mahmud, A. S., Miller, I. F., et al. (2022). Infectious disease in an era of global change.*Nature Reviews Microbiology,20* (4), 193-205.

Berman, E. P. (2022). Thinking like an economist: How efficiency replaced equality in US public policy. Princeton, NJ: Princeton University Press.

Biddle, L., Wahedi, K., Bozorgmehr, K. (2020). Health system resilience: a literature review of empirical research.*Health policy and planning35* (8) 1084-1109.

Brinkerhoff, D.W., Cross,H.E.,SharmaS.,et al. (2019) Stewardship and health systems strengthening: An overview.*Public Admin Dev39*:4–10.

Chan, J. C., Lim, L. L., Wareham, N. J., et al. (2020). The Lancet Commission on diabetes: using data to transform diabetes care and patient lives.*The Lancet396* (10267): 2019-2082.

Crawford, A. M., Shiferaw, A. A., Ntambwe, P., et al. (2023). Global critical care: a call to action.*Critical Care,27* (1), 28.

de Vries, N., Boone, A., Godderis, et al. (2023). The Race to Retain Healthcare Workers: A Systematic Review on Factors that Impact Retention of Nurses and Physicians in Hospitals.*Inquiry. 60*: 469580231159318.

Dickman, S. L., Himmelstein, D. U., Woolhandler, S. (2017). Inequality and the health-care system in the USA.*The Lancet,389* (10077), 1431-1441.

Duplechan, L. (2022) How health care organizations can be stewardship leaders. *AMA J Ethics* 24 (10): e1013-e1021.

Ebi, K. L., Vanos, J., Baldwin, J. W., et al. (2021). Extreme weather and climate change: population health and health system implications. *Annual review of public health,42* (1), 293-315.

Eckelman, M., et al. (2020) Health Care Pollution and Public Health Damage in the United States: An Update.*Health Affairs.* 39 (12): 2071–79.

Feagin, J., Bennefield, Z. (2014). Systemic racism and US health care. *Social science&medicine.103*: 7-14.

Ferguson, A., Ward, K., Parke, R. (2024). What is known about resilient healthcare systems in the context of natural disasters? A scoping review. *Collegian* https://doi.org/10.1016/j.colegn.2024.05.007.

Horowitz, J. M., Igielnik, R., Kochhar, R. (2020). Most Americans say there is too much economic inequality in the US, but fewer than half call it a top priority.*Pew Research Center,9.*

Huggel, C., Bouwer, L.M., Juhola, S.*et al.*(2022) The existential risk space of climate change.*Climatic Change***174**, 8.

Lal, A., Erondu, N. A., Heymann, D. L., et al. (2021). Fragmented health systems in COVID-19: rectifying the misalignment between global health security and universal health coverage. *The Lancet,397* (10268), 61-67.

Laprise, C. (2023). It's time to take a sustainable approach to health care in the face of the challenges of the 21st century.*One Health*16: 100510.

Li, W., Chai, Y., Khan, F., et al. (2021). A comprehensive survey on machine learning-based big data analytics for IoT-enabled smart healthcare system.*Mobile networks and applications,26*, 234-252.

Lopes, L., Montero, A., Presiado, M., et al. (2024) Americans' Challenges with Health Care Costs. *KFF Brief.* Access at https://www.kff.org/health-costs/issue-brief/americans-challenges-with-health-care-costs/.

Lugten, E.,& Hariharan, N. (2022). Strengthening Health Systems for Climate Adaptation and Health Security: Key Considerations for Policy and Programming.*Health security20* (5): 435–439.

Metzl, J. M., Maybank, A., De Maio, F. (2020). Responding to the COVID-19 pandemic: the need for a structurally competent health care system.*JAMA324* (3): 231-232.

Nasiri, T., Takian, A.,& Yazdani, S. (2019) Stewardship in Health, Designing a Multi-Layer Meta Model: A Review Article.*Iranian journal of public health48* (4): 579–592.

National Academies of Sciences, Engineering, and Medicine. (2021) Learning from Rapid Response, Innovation, and Adaptation to the COVID-19 Crisis: Proceedings of a Workshop in Brief. Washington, DC: The National Academies Press.

Niles, N. J. (2023).*Basics of the US health care system.* Burlington, MA: Jones& Bartlett Learning.

Nzinga, J., Boga, M., Kagwanja, N., et al. (2021). An innovative leadership development initiative to support building everyday resilience in health systems.*Health policy and planning36* (7): 1023-1035.

Okafor, C.M., Kolade, A., Onunka, T., et al. (2023) Mitigating cybersecurity risks in U.S. healthcare sector. IJRSI. 10 (9): 177-194.

Palagyi, A., Marais, B., Abimbola, S., et al. (2019) Health system preparedness for emerging infectious diseases: A synthesis of the literature. *Global Public Health* 14 (12): 1847-1868.

Seervai, S., Gustafsson, L., Abrams, M.K. (2022) How the U.S. Health Care System Contributes to Climate Change *Commonwealth Fund*. Accessed at https://www.commonwealthfund.org/publications/explainer/2022/apr/how-us-health-care- system- contributes-climate-change.

Shams, L., Sari, A. A., Yazdani, S., Nasiri, T. (2021). Model for Value-based Policy-making in Health Systems.*International journal of preventive medicine12*: 13.

Stanford F. C. (2020). The Importance of Diversity and Inclusion in the Healthcare Workforce.*Journal of the National Medical Association,112* (3), 247–249.

Thomas, S., Sagan, A., Larkin, J., et al. (2020). Strengthening health systems resilience: key concepts and strategies. Copenhagen, Denmark: European Observatory on Health Systems and Policies.

Vodovotz, Y., Barnard, N., Hu, F. B., et al. (2020). Prioritized research for the prevention, treatment, and reversal of chronic disease: recommendations from the lifestyle medicine research summit. *Frontiers in medicine7*: 585744.

Witter, S., Thomas, S., Topp, S. M., et al. (2023). Health system resilience: a critical review and reconceptualisation.*The Lancet Global Health,11* (9), e1454-e1458.

Wong, L., Qureshi, K., Glauberman, G., et al. (2022). Rapid Response: The Development of Just-in-Time Education for Nursing Clinicians and Students.*Hawai'i journal of health& social welfare*, 81 (1): 21–24.

Yearby, R., Clark, B., Figueroa, J. F. (2022) Structural Racism in Historical and Modern U. S. Health Care Policy. Health Affairs 41 (2): 187-194.

CHAPTER 2

HEALTHCARE STEWARDSHIP IN A MODERN-DAY SOCIETY

2.1 THE ROOTS OF STEWARDSHIP

Stewardship has its roots in biblical times. According to Saltman and Ferroussier-Davis (2000), the Old Testament presents the following references to stewardship:

- In Genesis, men and women were created in the image of God, given a privileged place among creatures, and commanded by God to exercise stewardship over the earth.

- Also in Genesis, Jacob's son, Joseph, when sold into slavery by his brothers becomes Potiphar's then Pharaoh's steward, and exhibits the following qualities of stewardship:

- He becomes a selfless servant of his masters.

- He manages his master's assets without owning any of them.

He anticipates the future trends and devises grand plans for the use of his master's assets.

In the New Testament, Jesus tells the parable of the talents, whereby a master divides his goods between his three servants. The story emphasizes that when one is entrusted with something of value by others, one has an obligation ethically and morally to improve the value of what they are managing. The notion of stewardship as an ethically driven responsibility for protecting and developing one's resources lies at the heart of both the Christian and Jewish faiths.

Saltman and Ferroussier-Davis (2000) describe the very first reference to health care stewardship based on religious teachings. The Islamic faith and the institution of Hisba organized public administrative functions in both the moral/normative and administrative/technical dimensions. The head of Al Hisba, the first Muhtasib, was appointed in Medina in the ninth century. The functions of the Muhtasib in precolonial Arab societies included the regulation of medical practice and pharmaceuticals and overseeing the requirements regarding the equitable provision of services and the public interest.

Religion also serves as the basis for the environmental and ecological stewardship that has emerged in Europe and North America within the past decade (Saltman and Ferroussier-Davis 2000). Originally, it started out as accountability to God in the Judeo-Christian doctrine. Responsibility to God has been replaced within the ecological and environmental movement with intergenerational responsibility. Saltman and Ferroussier-Davis (2000) interpret the lack of control over the degradation of the environment over centuries as humans' misinterpretation of God's mandate to be earth's steward as a license to dominate, exploit, and destroy the environment. Others argue that damage to the environment has occurred because of people disregarding God's recommendations to appropriately manage the earth's precious resources.

2.2 HEALTHCARE STEWARDSHIP DEFINED

Healthcare stewardship refers to the responsible management and utilization of limited healthcare resources (i.e., goods and services) to ensure the sustainability, efficiency, and effectiveness of healthcare delivery. It involves a broad range of activities aimed at optimizing health outcomes, improving the quality of care, and ensuring equitable access to healthcare services. The concept emphasizes the need for healthcare systems to operate in a manner that balances resource allocation, ethical considerations, and long-term planning to meet the current and future health needs of the US population (Brinkerhoff et al., 2019).

At its core, healthcare stewardship is about making informed decisions that promote the best possible health outcomes while minimizing waste and inefficiencies. This includes the prudent use of financial resources, medical supplies, and human capital, as well as the implementation of policies and practices that support the health and well-being of individuals and communities. Effective stewardship requires collaboration among various stakeholders, including government agencies, healthcare providers, patients, and the community, to ensure that resources are used judiciously and that the healthcare system remains resilient and responsive to changing needs.

Healthcare stewardship also encompasses the ethical obligation to provide high-quality care while addressing disparities and ensuring that all individuals have access to necessary services. This involves prioritizing interventions based on their effectiveness and cost-efficiency, promoting proactive care, and fostering a culture of accountability and continuous improvement within healthcare organizations. By emphasizing transparency, accountability, and the responsible use of resources, healthcare stewardship aims to build trust and confidence in the healthcare system, ultimately leading to better health outcomes for all.

In addition, healthcare stewardship is increasingly relevant in the context of global health challenges, such as pandemics, aging populations, and the rising burden of chronic diseases. As healthcare systems face these complex issues, the principles of stewardship guide the development of innovative solutions, the adoption of evidence-based practices, and the alignment of healthcare policies with broader societal goals. By focusing on sustainable and equitable healthcare delivery, stewardship ensures that health systems are not only prepared to address current challenges but are also resilient enough to adapt to future demands.

2.3 THE CORE PRINCIPLES OF HEALTHCARE STEWARDSHIP

Healthcare stewardship is underpinned by several core principles that guide the responsible management and utilization of healthcare resources. These principles aim to ensure that healthcare systems operate efficiently, ethically, and sustainably to meet the needs of the population (Kapoor et al., 2014).

One of the primary principles of healthcare stewardship is the efficient and effective use of limited resources. This involves optimizing the allocation of financial, human, and material resources to maximize health outcomes. Efficient healthcare systems focus on reducing waste, eliminating redundancies, and streamlining processes to ensure that resources are used where they can have the greatest impact. This includes implementing evidence-based practices, promoting proactive and personalized health care, and using data analytics to inform decision-making and improve patient care (Abrams et al., 2021).

Equity and accessibility are fundamental to healthcare stewardship (White-Williams et al., 2022). Ensuring that all individuals have fair access to healthcare services, regardless of their socioeconomic status, geographic location, or other determinants, is essential for achieving health equity. This principle emphasizes the need to address disparities in healthcare access and outcomes by removing barriers and providing targeted support to underserved and vulnerable populations. Policies and practices that promote inclusive healthcare, such as expanding insurance coverage, enhancing primary care services, and addressing social determinants of health, are critical to this principle.

Accountability and transparency are crucial for building trust and maintaining public confidence in the healthcare system (Meagher et al., 2022). Healthcare stewardship requires that healthcare providers, organizations, and policymakers be transparent, truthful, and accountable for their decisions and actions. This involves setting clear standards, monitoring performance, and ensuring that resources are used appropriately and ethically. Transparency in healthcare decision-making processes, resource allocation, and outcome reporting helps to foster accountability and allows stakeholders to assess the effectiveness and fairness of the healthcare system.

Sustainability is a key principle of healthcare stewardship, focusing on the long-term viability of healthcare systems (Hu et al., 2022). This involves balancing the immediate needs of the population with the preservation of resources for future generations. Sustainable healthcare practices include investing in proactive care, promoting healthy lifestyles, and adopting environmentally friendly practices within healthcare facilities. By prioritizing sustainability, healthcare systems can ensure that they remain resilient and capable of adapting to future challenges, such as demographic shifts, technological advancements, and emerging health threats.

Ethical considerations are integral to healthcare stewardship, guiding the fair and just distribution of resources and ensuring respect for patient rights and autonomy (Guidolin et al., 2022). This principle involves making decisions based on ethical frameworks that consider the needs and values of individuals and communities. Ethical stewardship includes respecting patient confidentiality, obtaining informed consent, and ensuring that care is provided in a manner that respects the dignity and rights of all patients. It also involves addressing ethical dilemmas, such as resource allocation during crises, through transparent and inclusive decision-making processes.

Effective healthcare stewardship requires collaboration and partnership among various stakeholders, including government agencies, healthcare providers, patients, and communities (Robu et al., 2020). This principle emphasizes the importance of working together to achieve common goals and improve health outcomes. Collaborative efforts can enhance resource sharing, promote the exchange of best practices, and foster innovation in healthcare delivery. Partnerships with community organizations, academic institutions, and international bodies can also help address complex health challenges and ensure a coordinated and comprehensive approach to healthcare stewardship.

2.4 WHAT ARE THE DRIVING FORCES BEHIND HEALTHCARE STEWARDSHIP?

Previously defined, *Healthcare Stewardship* refers to the responsible management and utilization of limited healthcare resources to achieve optimal health outcomes for individuals and populations. It involves the careful planning, regulation, and oversight of healthcare systems to ensure efficiency, equity, quality, and sustainability. Several driving forces underpin healthcare stewardship, shaping principles, policies, practices, and the overall approach to healthcare management. These forces can be broadly categorized into economic, social, political, and technological factors (He et al., 2022; Wilson et al., 2020; Kaiser et al., 2022; Tello et al., 2020; Scott et al., 2021; Hubbard et al., 2022; Dion et al., 2024; MacNeill et al., 2021; Fatemi et al., 2022; Shaw et al., 2021).

1. Economic Factors

    a. Cost Containment: Rising healthcare costs are a major concern for governments, insurers, and patients. Effective stewardship aims to control the total costs of care without compromising patient quality and safety by promoting efficient use of resources, reducing waste, and implementing cost-effective interventions.

    b. Resource Allocation: Ensuring that resources are distributed equitably to meet the needs of different population groups is critical. This includes prioritizing primary care services at both the individual and population socio-ecological levels of organization and the most cost-effective interventions that maximize patient health outcomes.

    c. Value-Based Care: Emphasizing value over volume, this approach focuses on achieving better health outcomes per dollar spent, incentivizing providers to deliver high-quality, safe, timely, effective, efficacious, and equitable patient-centered care.

2. Social Factors

   a. Health Equity: closing health disparities in access and navigation to appropriate medical care is a key goal of healthcare stewardship. This involves ensuring that vulnerable and marginalized populations receive evidence-based medical care in-person or by telehealth and that all determinants of health are addressed.

   b. Population Health Management: Focusing on the health outcomes of entire populations rather than just individual patients, stewardship efforts aim to improve community health status through health prevention, health promotion, health protection, health preparedness (i.e., P⁴ Health), coordinated medical care with essential public health services, and community health worker navigation assistance from community-based organizations for chronic conditions.

   c. People-Centered Care: Engaging people in their own care towards self-efficacy and self-actualization and ensuring that healthcare services are responsive to their cultural needs, preferences and values is essential for effective stewardship.

3. Political Factors

   a. Regulation and Oversight: Governments play a critical role in regulating healthcare systems, setting standards for quality, safety, and ethics, and ensuring compliance through monitoring and enforcement.

   b. Policy and Legislation: Healthy public policies and laws shape the structure and functioning of healthcare systems. Effective stewardship requires sound policy-making that is informed by evidence and aimed at achieving equitable and efficient healthcare delivery.

   c. Public Accountability: Ensuring transparency and accountability in healthcare decisions and spending is foundational to healthcare stewardship. This includes involving stakeholders in decision-making processes and regularly reporting on healthcare performance and outcomes that matter the most to patients. Use of real-time dashboards and annual scorecards are examples of tools that transparently present healthcare outcomes in different formats for different purposes for different populations.

4. Technological Factors

    a. Health Information Technology: The use of electronic health records (EHRs), telemedicine, and health information exchanges (HIEs) enhances the efficiency, quality, and coordination of care. Effective stewardship involves leveraging these technologies to capitalize on the interoperability of current information systems to improve health outcomes by using encounter/claims-based data with EHR-derived clinical information and streamline healthcare processes.

    b. Innovation and Research: Investing in medical research, establishing learning health systems, and encouraging innovation in healthcare practices and advanced technologies can lead to improved treatments and more efficient and effective medical care delivery. Stewardship involves supporting and regulating these innovations to ensure they benefit individuals and the public-at-large.

    c. Data Analytics: Utilizing big data, computational science, systems medicine and advanced analytics to inform provider and patient decision-making, track health outcomes, and identify areas for closing health disparities is a key aspect of modern healthcare stewardship.

5. Ethical and Moral Factors

    a. Ethical Decision-Making: Ensuring that healthcare decisions are made ethically with cultural humility and empathy considering the health, wellness, and well-being of patients. Reasonableness and social justice for both individuals and the community-at-large are also of importance in healthcare decision-making. This includes making difficult choices about resource allocation and prioritizing interventions based on well-established ethical principles.

    b. Patient Rights: Upholding patient rights to informed consent, privacy, and autonomy is crucial. Effective stewardship involves protecting these rights while striving to achieve the best health outcomes.

6. Environmental Factors

    a. Sustainable Practices: Promoting environmentally sustainable practices within healthcare systems, such as reducing waste, conserving energy, and using eco-friendly materials, is increasingly recognized as part of responsible stewardship.

    b. Climate Change and Health: Addressing the health impacts of Anthropogenic climate change and preparing healthcare systems to respond to climate-related health threats are important components of modern healthcare stewardship.

    c. Nature-based Solutions: Considered to be a broad definition covering the conserving of biodiversity by society in a sustainable manner, while also integrating social factors such as socio-economic development and effective leadership and governance. Provide a range of eco-system services beneficial for the urban biosphere such as regulation of micro-climates, flood prevention, water treatment, food provision, and more.

Healthcare stewardship is driven by a complex interplay of economic, social, political, technological, ethical, and environmental factors. Effective stewardship aims to produce positive health, optimize wellness and well-being, improve health outcomes, ensure equity and access, control total costs of care, and promote sustainable and ethical healthcare practices. By addressing these driving forces, healthcare systems can better meet the needs of their populations and navigate the challenges of an evolving healthcare landscape.

2.5 THE POTENTIAL FOR IMPROVING HEALTHY PUBLIC POLICY WITH HEALTHCARE STEWARDSHIP

The positive aspect of stewardship links its potential for improving health policy outcomes (Saltman et al., 2000; Redvers, 2021; Woolhandler et al., 2021; Bak-Coleman et al., 2021). The main issue at the heart of this debate is the conundrum of focusing the health policy process on traditional principal-agent relationships creating economically stable health systems. It is possible, however, to create a health system that is not only cost-efficient or economically viable but is also good by stressing normative, ethically oriented expectations of stewardship.

Stewardship should serve as a guiding principle for power in health systems, prioritizing the common good over economic interests. Stewardship offers the prospect of refreshing the sense of collective impact and social justice among the stakeholders of a health system. This may ultimately lead to a restoration of trust, truthfulness, and legitimacy between a health system and the population it serves. It is important to note, however, that stewardship appears to be most compatible with a broadly multicultural society. Unpopular decisions securing the underlying best interests of the population served by a health system are truly at the core of the most basic principles of health care stewardship. This may or may not allow for a smooth, linear ascent to improving health care outcomes Constant vigilance is required to identify competing self-interests among the stakeholders of the health system. This effort aligns with one of the core functions of stewardship: building partnerships. The real potential for stewardship in health care delivery lies in its attempt to bring back in modern form the idea of the *commons*, a collective set of values (Cassel et al., 2007; Hiatt, 1975, Hardin, 1968). At the core of health care stewardship is a social contract between the health system and the population served by the health system. It is this social contract, tied to a collective set of values, the "commons," that allows stewardship to move beyond issues of cost efficiency and market-oriented health economics. In essence, stewardship can establish a more socially responsible, normative framework focused on achieving socially-desirable health outcomes.

A stewardship approach, based in developing the collective health commons, fits well with the mission of providing sound clinical services by health care providers. For physicians, this mission-oriented framework lies at the core of the Hippocratic Oath. The concept of health care stewardship is also consistent with evidence-based medicine and empirically-supported clinical practice guidelines. Grounded in both ethical and economic norms, the healthcare delivery strategy based on stewardship can provide the available evidence about what works well to support population-based measures that can improve overall health, wellness, and well-being.

Applying the principles of healthcare stewardship to present-day issues facing health systems creates the careful, well-constructed opportunity of managing limited health care resources in a transparent, accountable, and socially-responsible manner. Stewardship applies economically-driven interests in the delivery of health care goods and services by balancing those interests with an ethically normative collection of values (i.e., the medical commons). This allows for the overall health, wellness, and well-being of the population being served by the health system to take priority, while the health system fulfills its operational, political, and social mission and vision. There is much more work to be done in the quantitative assessment of stewardship function. Additional research and identification of other domains that fully delineate stewardship activity is indicated.

2.6 REFERENCES

Abrams, E. M., Singer, A. G., Shaker, M., et al. (2021). What the COVID-19 pandemic can teach us about resource stewardship and quality in health care.*The Journal of Allergy and Clinical Immunology: In Practice9* (2): 608-612.

Brinkerhoff, D.W., Cross,H.E.,SharmaS.,et al. (2019) Stewardship and health systems strengthening: An overview.*Public Admin Dev*39:4–10.

Cassel, C. K, and T. E. Brennan. 2007. Managing medical resources: Return to the commons? *JAMA* 297 (22): 2518–2521.

Dion, H., Evans, M. (2024). Strategic frameworks for sustainability and corporate governance in healthcare facilities; approaches to energy-efficient hospital management.*Benchmarking: An International Journal*31 (2): 353-390.

Fatemi, Y., Bergl, P. A. (2022). Diagnostic stewardship: Appropriate testing and judicious treatments.*Critical Care Clinics*38 (1): 69-87.

Guidolin, K., Catton, J., Rubin, B., et al. (2022) Ethical decision making during a healthcare crisis: a resource allocation framework and tool.*Journal of Medical Ethics* 48 (8): 504-509.

Hardin, G. (1968) Tragedy of the Commons. Science 162 (3859): 1243-1248.

He, A. J., Bali, A. S., Ramesh, M. (2022). Active stewardship in healthcare: Lessons from China's health policy reforms.*Social Policy& Administration* 56 (6), 925-940.

Hiatt, H.H. (1975) Protecting the Medical Commons: Who Is Responsible? New England Journal of Medicine, 293, 235-241.

Hu, H., Cohen, G., Sharma, B., et al. (2022). Sustainability in health care.*Annual Review of Environment and Resources*47 (1): 173-196.

Hubbard, R., Paquet, G., Wilson, C. (2022).*Stewardship: Collaborative Decentred Metagovernance and Inquiring Systems.* Ottawa, Canada: University of Ottawa Press.

Kaiser, R. A., Taing, L., Bhatia, H. (2022) Antimicrobial resistance and environmental health: a water stewardship framework for global and national action *Antibiotics* 11 (1): 63.

Kapoor, N., Kumar, D., Thakur, N. (2014). Core attributes of stewardship; foundation of sound health system.*International journal of health policy and management3* (1): 5–6.

MacNeill, A. J., McGain, F., Sherman, J. D. (2021). Planetary health care: a framework for sustainable health systems.*The Lancet Planetary Health5* (2): e66-e68.

Meagher, K. M., Watson, S., Suh, G. A.,& Virk, A. (2022). The new precision stewards? *Journal of Personalized Medicine12* (8): 1308.

Redvers, N. (2021). Patient-planetary health co-benefit prescribing: emerging considerations for health policy and health professional practice.*Frontiers in Public Health9*: 678545.

Robu, D., Lazar, J. B. (2020). Shaping Successful Stakeholder Engagement by Design: Digital Transformation in Healthcare. *In*European Conference on Knowledge Management. Academic Conferences International Limited.

Saltman, R. B., and O. Ferroussier-Davis. (2000) The concept of stewardship in health policy. *Bulletin of the World Health Organization* 78 (6): 732–739.

Scott, R. E., Morris, C., Mars, M. (2021) Development of a "cellphone stewardship framework": legal, regulatory, and ethical issues. *Telemedicine and e-Health27* (3): 316-322.

Shaw, E., Walpole, S., McLean, M., et al. (2021). AMEE Consensus Statement: Planetary health and education for sustainable healthcare.*Medical Teacher43* (3): 272-286.

Tello, J. E., Barbazza, E., Waddell, K. (2020). Review of 128 quality of care mechanisms: A framework and mapping for health system stewards.*Health Policy124* (1): 12-24.

White-Williams, C., Bittner, V., Eagleson, R., et al. (2022). Interprofessional collaborative practice improves access to care and healthcare quality to advance health equity. *The Journal for Healthcare Quality (JHQ)* 44 (5), 294-304.

Wilson, T., Bevan, G., Gray, M., et al. (2020) Developing a culture of stewardship: how to prevent the Tragedy of the Commons in universal health systems. *Journal of the Royal Society of Medicine* 113 (7): 255-261.

Woolhandler, S., Himmelstein, D. U., Ahmed, S., et al. (2021) Public policy and health in the Trump era. *The Lancet* 397 (10275): 705-753.

CHAPTER 3

FOUNDATIONAL PILLARS, CAPACITY BUILDING, AND SUSTAINABILITY IN HEALTHCARE STEWARDSHIP

3.1 CHALLENGES FACING HEALTHCARE STEWARDSHIP

Healthcare stewardship faces numerous challenges that can impede the effective management and utilization of limited healthcare resources.

1. Resource Limitations

    a. Funding Constraints: Limited financial resources can restrict the availability of essential healthcare services and medications, particularly in low-income countries or underserved areas. Budget cuts and economic downturns further exacerbate these issues.

    b. Workforce Shortages: A shortage of healthcare professionals, including doctors, nurses, and allied health workers, can lead to increased workloads, burnout, and decreased quality of care.

2. Inequitable Access

   a. Disparities in Healthcare: All determinants of health, such as income, education, housing stability, food security, transportation, and geographic location, can lead to significant disparities in access and navigation to healthcare services. Marginalized and vulnerable populations often face extreme obstacles and barriers to receiving high-quality and safe medical care.

   b. Rural and Remote Areas: Providing healthcare services in rural and remote areas can be challenging due to logistical issues, lack of infrastructure, and a smaller well-trained healthcare workforce.

3. Policy and Governance Issues

   a. Inconsistent Policies: Variability in healthcare policies across regions or countries can create confusion and inefficiencies in the delivery of care. Inconsistent regulations can also hinder the implementation of best clinical practices.

   b. Corruption and Mismanagement: Corruption and mismanagement of healthcare funding and resources can lead to fraud, waste and abuse of funds and resources, reduced quality and safety of care, and decreased trust in the healthcare system.

4. Technological Barriers

   a. Digital Divide: The adoption of health information technology, such as electronic health records (EHRs), SMART devices, broad-band access, and telemedicine can be hampered by a lack of digital infrastructure and technical expertise, particularly in low-resource settings.

   b. Personal Security Concerns: Protecting patient privacy and identifiable information and ensuring the security of healthcare systems from cyber threats is a growing challenge as reliance on digital tools increases.

c. Interoperability: Improving the ability of health information technology and systems to access and communicate bi-directionally in a coordinated and meaningful manner between independent healthcare entities.

5. Resistance to Change

   a. Cultural and Organizational Resistance: Healthcare organizations and providers may resist changes to established medical practices and clinical protocols, hindering the adoption of new, evidence-based, empirically-supported approaches to medical care.

   b. Patient Non-Adherence: Ensuring patient adherence to treatment plans for chronic conditions and disease prevention with early detection and screening measures can be difficult, impacting health outcomes and resource utilization.

6. Public Health Emergencies

   a. Pandemics and Epidemics: Public health emergencies, such as epidemics, pandemics, and endemics place immense strain on integrated and comprehensive medical care and essential public health services and functions leading to resource shortages, overwhelmed facilities, and increased morbidity and mortality.

   b. Natural Disasters: Natural disasters can disrupt healthcare services, damage infrastructure, and create urgent healthcare needs that challenge existing resources and capabilities.

7. Moral and Ethical Dilemmas

   a. Resource Allocation Decisions: Making decisions about how to allocate limited resources, such as during organ transplantation or in the distribution of scarce medications, raises ethical dilemmas and requires careful consideration of justice and equity.

b. Balancing Cost and Quality: Ensuring that cost-saving measures do not compromise the quality and safety of healthcare services is a persistent challenge in healthcare stewardship.

8. Global Health Issues

a. Cross-Border Health Threats: Emerging infectious diseases and other health communicable disease threats that cross national borders require coordinated international health system responses, which can be difficult to achieve due to differing multi-level priorities and capabilities.

b. Health Inequities: Addressing global health inequities and ensuring that all populations have access to necessary basic healthcare services is a complex and ongoing challenge.

These challenges highlight the need for continuous efforts to improve healthcare stewardship through creative and innovative solutions, collaboration and cooperation among stakeholders, and the development of robust healthy public policies and practices that promote the sustainable and equitable use of healthcare resources.

3.2 FOUNDATIONAL PILLARS OF HEALTHCARE STEWARDSHIP

Healthcare stewardship involves the responsible planning and management of limited health resources (Lear et al., 2016). The foundational characteristics of healthcare stewardship are many. First, transparency and accountability are necessary to earn trust in those being served with medical care. It is critical to ensure that all healthcare stakeholders including health care providers, administrators, and policymakers are answerable for their actions and decisions. It is imperative that transparent structures and processes for resource allocation and decision-making are implemented with cultural humility and empathy. Clear and truthful lines of communication about policies, procedures, and outcomes and providing all stakeholders with access to information on how resources are used and decisions are made is crucial for delivering healthcare services. Second, moral and ethical decision-making ensures that medical care decisions are made based on ethical healthcare principles such as justice, autonomy, beneficence, and non-maleficence. Prioritizing patient health, safety, and welfare (HSW) and closing health disparities (e.g., health equity) in the delivery of healthcare goods and services is also critical for improving healthcare outcomes. Third, operational efficiency and cost-effectiveness in the delivery of healthcare services is both necessary and sufficient to optimize appropriate resource use to maximize health outcomes while reducing fraud, waste and abuse. Fourth, ensuring that healthcare practices and resource use are sustainable over the long term for present and future generations of patients should be a part of any strategic plan. Also, considering the environmental, economic, commercial, and social determinates of health and their collective impact on individuals and communities provides a 360-degree view of the upstream needs for individuals and the public-at-large. Fifth, quality improvement science should play a major role in continuously seeking to improve the quality and safety of healthcare services with empirically-derived quality improvement tools, implementing empirically-derived, evidence-based practices and encouraging disruptive innovation in healthcare service areas of most need. Sixth, ensuring that all individuals have access to the healthcare services they need, prefer, and value regardless of their socio-economic status, ethnicity, or geographic location is critical to addressing health disparities, health literacy, and promoting inclusive healthy public policies. Seventh, the 5 C's, collaboration, cooperation, coordination, communication and capacity building are sufficient and necessary among various stakeholders, including government agencies, healthcare providers, patients, and communities. This enables the promoting of cross-disciplinary discourse and action to address broader determinants of health using socio-ecological framework at macro, meso, and micro levels of organization. Next, establishing robust regulatory and statutory frameworks to oversee healthcare practices and ensure compliance with the highest quality standards in mind for individuals and populations served. Implementing effective leadership and governance structures and processes to manage healthcare systems ensure transparency, accountability, and truthfulness leading to long-term trusting relationships within the service community. Lastly, people-centered care, focusing on the needs, preferences, and values of patients, their families and the communities where they work, live and play with cultural humility and empathy, lead to positive relationships involving patients in shared decision-making processes and respecting their autonomy.

These characteristics help ensure that healthcare delivery systems operate safely, efficiently, effectively, ethically, and sustainably; ultimately leading to a population health management strategy with holistic, integrated and comprehensive medical care that will ensure better health outcomes for individuals, their families and the communities where they live, work and play.

3.3   BUILDING   CAPACITY   INTO   HEALTHCARE STEWARDSHIP

Building capacity in people, processes, and technology related to healthcare stewardship involves a strategic approach to enhance skills, improve systems, and leverage technological advancements (Anderson et al., 2020; McDarby et al., 2022; Milstein et al, 2020; Nasiri et al., 2021). Here are key steps for each area.

1. People
    a. Training and Education:
        1. Develop and implement training programs that focus on healthcare stewardship principles, ethical decision-making, and medical supply chain management.
        2. Offer continuing education opportunities for healthcare professionals to stay updated with best practices, emerging trends, and advancing technology.

b. Leadership Development:

   1. Identify and mentor potential leaders within the healthcare system.

   2. Provide leadership training that emphasizes strategic and critical thinking, transparency, accountability, integrity, and ethical stewardship.

   3. Hard and soft skill education and training is foundational to leadership training.

c. Interdisciplinary Collaboration:

   1. Encourage inter-disciplinary teamwork and communication among different research scientists and healthcare professionals.

   2. Facilitate cross-disciplinary workshops, pod-casts, and seminars to foster collaborative problem-solving, creativity, and innovation.

d. Mentorship and Support:

   1. Establish mentorship programs where experienced professionals guide and support less experienced colleagues.

   2. Establish learning healthcare systems (i.e., macro) and communities of practice (i.e., micro) for sharing knowledge and resources.

2. Process

a. Standardization and Best Practices:

   1. Develop standardized operations, clinical policies, protocols, and guidelines based on empirically-supported evidence-based best practices.

   2. Regularly review and update operations, clinical policies, protocols, and guidelines to reflect current research and technological advancements.

b. Quality Improvement Initiatives:

1. Implement continuous quality improvement (CQI) processes to identify, analyze, and improve healthcare practices.

2. Use principles of QI science to provide a working framework to help guide initiatives and innovation.

c. Performance Measurement and Monitoring:

   1. Design and implement key performance indicators (KPIs) to monitor and evaluate healthcare processes.

   2. Use data analytics to identify areas for improvement and track progress over time.

   3. Establish just-in-time dashboards and annual performance scorecards to establish a transparent, accountable, and truthful environment.

d. Effective Communication:

   1. Develop clear, factual-based communication channels both internal and external to current work environment.

   2. Use regular meetings, reports, and digital communication tools to ensure everyone is informed and aligned to the mission and vision of organization.

3. Technology

   a. Health Information Systems (HIS):

      1. Implement robust health information systems to manage patient data, streamline clinical workflows, and improve decision-making.

      2. Execute data sharing and privacy agreements to allow the flow of sensitive and personal patient data.

      3. Ensure interoperability between different systems to facilitate seamless data exchange.

b. Telehealth and Remote Monitoring:

1. Establish free broad-band internet capabilities to close the digital divide.

2. Utilize telehealth technologies to expand access to care, especially in underserved areas.

3. Implement remote monitoring tools to track patient health and provide timely interventions for patients with chronic conditions

c. Data Analytics and Artificial Intelligence (AI):

1. Leverage data analytics to gain insights into healthcare trends, outcomes, and resource utilization.

2. Use AI and machine learning to predict patient outcomes, optimize treatments, and identify inefficiencies.

d. Cybersecurity:

1. Ensure robust cybersecurity measures to protect patient health information and maintain personal privacy.

2. Regularly update security protocols and conduct training on data protection for all staff annually and as needed.

4. Integrative Approach

a. Stakeholder Engagement:

1. Involve all stakeholders, including healthcare providers, patients, policymakers, and the community, in capacity-building initiatives.

2. Gather input and feedback to ensure that efforts are relevant and effective.

b. Resource Allocation:

1. Allocate all resources (i.e., financial, human, and technological) strategically to areas with the highest need to achieve high-quality and safe patient care.

2. Ensure that investments in advanced medical technology and training are aligned with organizational goals and healthcare priorities.

c. Healthy Public Policy Development:

1. Develop and implement healthy public policies that support healthcare stewardship, including regulations, funding mechanisms, and incentives.

2. Advocate for all policies to promote sustainable practices and equitable access to healthcare.

By focusing on these areas, healthcare organizations can build capacity in people, processes, and technology, leading to more effective stewardship and better health outcomes.

3.4 SUSTAINABILITY IN HEALTHCARE STEWARDSHIP

Sustainability in healthcare stewardship refers to the responsible management of limited healthcare resources to ensure the long-term viability of healthcare systems while minimizing environmental impact (Enqvist et al., 2018). This involves implementing practices that balance economic efficiency, social equity, and environmental protection. Key aspects of sustainable healthcare stewardship include reducing waste, conserving energy, and promoting the use of sustainable materials. Hospitals and healthcare facilities are increasingly adopting green building standards, such as LEED certification, to reduce their carbon footprint and improve energy efficiency. Additionally, implementing waste reduction programs, such as recycling medical supplies and properly disposing of hazardous materials, plays a critical role in promoting environmental sustainability (Sherman et al., 2020).

Another important facet of sustainability in healthcare is the adoption of sustainable procurement practices. This involves sourcing medical supplies, equipment, and pharmaceuticals from suppliers who adhere to environmentally friendly and socially responsible practices. By prioritizing products that are biodegradable, recyclable, or have a lower environmental impact, healthcare organizations can significantly reduce their ecological footprint. Furthermore, fostering partnerships with suppliers committed to sustainability can drive innovation in the production of green medical technologies and supplies (Handfield et al., 2020).

Healthcare stewardship also encompasses the efficient use of financial resources to ensure the long-term sustainability of healthcare services (Brinkerhoff et al., 2019). This involves implementing value-based care models that focus on delivering high-quality care while controlling costs. By incentivizing preventive care and efficient resource utilization, these models help reduce unnecessary medical interventions and hospital readmissions, ultimately leading to cost savings and improved patient outcomes. Additionally, leveraging data analytics and health information technology can optimize resource allocation and enhance operational efficiency, further contributing to the sustainability of healthcare systems.

Community engagement and education are essential components of sustainable healthcare stewardship (Mitchell et al., 2022). Educating patients and communities about preventive care, healthy lifestyles, and the responsible use of healthcare services can reduce the overall demand for medical interventions and promote better health outcomes. Community health programs that address social determinants of health, such as access to nutritious food, safe housing, and education, are also crucial for fostering long-term health and well-being. By investing in community health and preventive care, healthcare organizations can create a more sustainable and resilient healthcare system.

Lastly, sustainability in healthcare stewardship requires a commitment to ongoing innovation and improvement (Bornbusch et al., 2014). This involves staying abreast of the latest advancements in medical research, technology, and practices that contribute to sustainability. Healthcare organizations must foster a culture of continuous learning and improvement, encouraging staff to adopt sustainable practices and embrace new technologies that enhance efficiency and reduce environmental impact. By prioritizing sustainability in all aspects of healthcare delivery, organizations can ensure the long-term health and well-being of both patients and the planet.

3.5 REFERENCES

Anderson, J. E., Ross, A. J., Macrae, C., et al. (2020) Defining adaptive capacity in healthcare: a new framework for researching resilient performance.*Applied Ergonomics*87: 103111.

Brinkerhoff, D. W., Cross, H. E., Sharma, S., et al. (2019) Stewardship and health systems strengthening: An overview.*Public Administration and Development*39 (1), 4-10.

Bornbusch, A., Dickens, T., Hart, C., et al. (2014). A stewardship approach to shaping the future of public health supply chain systems.*Global Health: Science and Practice* 2 (4): 403-409.

Enqvist, J. P., West, S., Masterson, V. A., et al. (2018) Stewardship as a boundary object for sustainability research: Linking care, knowledge and agency.*Landscape and urban planning*179: 17-37.

Handfield, R., Finkenstadt, D. J., Schneller, E. S., et al. (2020) A commons for a supply chain in the post-COVID-19 era: the case for a reformed strategic national stockpile.*The Milbank Quarterly*98 (4), 1058-1090.

Lear, J. L., Fleig-Palmer, M. M., Hodge, K. A., et al. (2016) Business fundamentals for healthcare providers: Ensuring effective practice management and good stewardship.*Journal of Health Administration Education* 33 (1): 141-162.

McDarby, G., Mustafa, S., Zhang, Y., et al. (2022) Essential Public Health Functions in Ireland: Perspectives to strengthen capacities and stewardship.*European Journal of Public Health*,32 (3): 129-207.

Milstein, B., Erickson, J., Gouveia, T., et al. (2020) Amplifying stewardship: characteristics and trends stewards consider when expanding equitable well-being. RWJF: The Ripple Foundation.

Mitchell, J., Cooke, P., Ahorlu, C., et al. (2022) Community engagement: The key to tackling Antimicrobial Resistance (AMR) across a One Health context? *Global Public Health*,17 (11): 2647-2664.

Nasiri, T., Yazdani, S., Shams, L., et al. (2021) Stewardship of noncommunicable diseases in Iran: a qualitative study. *International Journal of Health Governance* 26 (2): 179-198.

Sherman, J. D., Thiel, C., MacNeill, A., et al. (2020) The green print: advancement of environmental sustainability in healthcare. *Resources, Conservation and Recycling*161: 104882.

CHAPTER 4

A SHORT PRIMER ON THE AMERICAN HEALTHCARE DELIVERY SYSTEM

4.1 THE AMERICAN HEALTHCARE DELIVERY SYSTEM

The American healthcare delivery system is a complex, adaptive, and multileveled structure comprising various stakeholders, including patients, healthcare providers, insurance companies, and governmental bodies (Niles, 2023, Shi et al., 2014). At its core, healthcare delivery involves the provision of medical services to individuals through a network of hospitals, clinics, private practices, and specialized care centers. The system operates through both public and private sectors, with funding sourced from government programs like Medicare and Medicaid, employer-sponsored insurance plans, and out-of-pocket payments by individuals.

Healthcare providers in the U.S. range from primary care physicians to specialists, nurses, and allied health professionals. These providers deliver care across different settings, including inpatient, outpatient, and long-term care facilities. Primary care serves as the entry point for patients, offering disease prevention, health promotion, treatment of common illnesses and injuries, and management of chronic conditions.

When specialized care is needed, patients are referred to specialists who provide advanced treatments and procedures.

Insurance coverage plays a critical role in the American healthcare system, determining access to and affordability of care. The majority of Americans obtain health insurance through their employers, while others purchase individual plans or are covered by government programs. Medicare provides coverage for individuals aged 65 and older and some younger individuals with disabilities. Medicaid offers assistance to low-income individuals and families. Despite these programs, gaps in coverage remain, leading to disparities in access to healthcare services.

The American healthcare system is also characterized by its emphasis on medical technology and innovation. The U.S. is a leader in medical research and the development of new treatments and technologies. However, this focus on cutting-edge care often comes with high costs, contributing to the overall expense of the system. Efforts to control costs and improve efficiency have led to various reforms, including the Affordable Care Act (ACA), which aimed to expand insurance coverage and introduce measures to enhance care quality and reduce spending.

Overall, the American healthcare delivery system is a dynamic and evolving entity, striving to balance the provision of high-quality care with the challenges of accessibility, affordability, and sustainability. Its complexity requires continuous evaluation and reform to meet the diverse needs of its population.

4.2 COMPARING US HEALTHCARE DELIVERY TO HEALTHCARE DELIVERY IN OTHER HIGH-INCOME COUNTRIES

The American healthcare delivery system is often compared to those of other high-income countries due to its unique characteristics and outcomes (OECD, 2023). One of the most significant differences is the level of spending. The US spends substantially higher percentage of its GDP on healthcare than other high-income countries. Despite this high expenditure, the U.S. does not achieve commensurate outcomes in terms of life expectancy, infant mortality, and overall health status. The complexity and fragmentation of the U.S. system, characterized by a mix of public and private insurance, often result in higher administrative costs and less efficiency compared to more streamlined, universal systems found in countries like the UK, Canada, and Australia.

In contrast, many high-income countries provide universal healthcare through single-payer systems or regulated multi-payer systems that ensure all residents have access to necessary medical services. These systems generally result in lower overall healthcare costs per capita and better health outcomes. For example, the National Health Service (NHS) in the UK and the public healthcare system in Canada offer extensive coverage with minimal out-of-pocket costs for patients, funded largely through taxation. These systems prioritize preventive care and have robust primary care networks, which contribute to more effective management of chronic diseases and overall better population health.

Moreover, other high-income countries emphasize price regulation and negotiation for pharmaceuticals and medical services, which significantly lowers costs. In Germany and Switzerland, for instance, government and non-governmental bodies negotiate prices with providers and pharmaceutical companies, leading to more affordable care without compromising quality. The U.S., however, lacks such centralized bargaining power, often resulting in exorbitant prices for drugs and medical services, contributing to financial strain on individuals and the healthcare system as a whole.

Another point of comparison is the equity of healthcare access. In many high-income countries with universal systems, there is a stronger emphasis on equity, ensuring that all citizens, regardless of income or social status, receive a similar standard of care. The U.S. system, with its reliance on employer-based insurance and significant out-of-pocket costs, often results in disparities in access to care. This leads to variations in the quality of care received and health outcomes based on socioeconomic status, further exacerbating health inequities.

Overall, while the U.S. healthcare delivery system is notable for its advanced medical technology and innovative treatments, it faces challenges related to cost, efficiency, and equity when compared to other high-income countries. The experiences of these countries offer valuable lessons in achieving more affordable, equitable, and effective healthcare systems.

4.3 MEDICAL SERVICES IN AMERICAN HEALTHCARE DELIVERY SYSTEM

The American healthcare delivery system strives to become an integrated, holistic and comprehensive medical care delivery structure. This process begins with intentions to streamline the navigation and enhance the coordination of patient care across various healthcare settings and providers. This system focuses on providing holistic and comprehensive people-centered care that addresses the full spectrum of health needs from prevention, promotion, protection, and preparedness to acute and chronic disease management. Integration involves seamless cooperation, coordination, collaboration, and communication among primary care physicians, specialists, hospitals, and other healthcare entities to ensure continuity of care, reduce fraud, abuse, and waste, and improve health outcomes.

In an integrated healthcare system, electronic health records (EHRs) play a vital role in enabling efficient interoperability information sharing among providers. EHRs allow for real-time access to patient medical histories, test results, and treatment plans, facilitating informed and shared decision-making and minimizing the risk of preventable errors. This technological integration supports the comprehensive management of personalized medical care, ensuring that all providers involved in a patient's care are well-informed and aligned in their approach to provide healthcare services the patient needs, prefers, and values with cultural humility and empathy.

Comprehensive care within this system encompasses a wide range of services, including proactive care, acute care, chronic care with evidence-based disease management, mental health services, and palliative care. By addressing the diverse needs of patients throughout their lifespan, the system aims to improve overall health outcomes and enhance both an individual's quality and quantity of life. Routine empirically-supported detection and evidence-based screening for diseases in their sub-clinical stages are crucial for early identification and intervention. This approach helps to reduce the burden of disease and associated healthcare costs that become irreversible beyond a critical clinical threshold.

Another key component of an integrated, holistic, and comprehensive medical care system is the emphasis on patient-centered care. This approach prioritizes the cultural preferences, needs, and values of patients, involving them in a shared decision-making process and tailoring personalized care plans to their unique circumstances. Patient-centered care fosters stronger patient-provider relationships, enhances overall patient satisfaction, engages in the patient experience, and promotes better adherence to treatment plans. Additionally, integrated care models often incorporate multidisciplinary teams, including physicians, nurses, social workers, and other healthcare professionals, working together to provide holistic care that addresses the physical, emotional, and social aspects of health.

Furthermore, integrated, holistic, and comprehensive care systems often employ population health management strategies to address the needs of specific groups within the community. By analyzing population-focused data and identifying trends, healthcare providers can implement targeted interventions to improve health outcomes for vulnerable populations, such as those with chronic conditions or socio-economic challenges. This proactive approach aims to close health disparities and promote health equity across marginally and diverse communities.

Holistic medical care is an approach to health and wellness that considers the whole person—body, mind, spirit, and emotions—in the quest to produce positive health and optimize wellness and well-being. The primary goal of holistic medicine is to achieve positive health and optimized wellness and well-being by gaining proper balance in life. This method of care recognizes that each individual is unique, with different preferences, needs, and values which means treatment plans are often personalized. Instead of focusing solely on symptoms, holistic medicine looks at the root causes of illnesses injuries and promotes processes to attack these root causes leading to self-efficacy, self-management, and self-healing.

A central tenet of holistic medical care is the belief that unconditional love and support are powerful healers and that a person is ultimately responsible for their own health, wellness, and well-being. Practitioners of holistic medicine often incorporate a variety of treatment techniques to help their patients take responsibility for their own health and well-being and achieve optimized wellness. These may include conventional medicine, lifestyle changes, nutrition, physical fitness, spiritual counseling, and alternative therapies such as acupuncture, chiropractic care, homeopathy, massage therapy, and yoga.

Holistic medical care also emphasizes the patient-practitioner relationship. It encourages open communication and collaboration between the patient and healthcare provider, fostering a therapeutic partnership. This approach is not limited to treating diseases but extends to fostering overall health, wellness, and well-being with both quantity and quality of life. By addressing multiple aspects of an individual's life, holistic care aims to improve physical health, enhance emotional, and spiritual well-being.

In summary, the integrated, holistic, and comprehensive American medical care system seeks to provide cohesive, patient-centered care through enhanced coordination among providers, the use of advanced technology, and a focus on integrated, holistic, and comprehensive health services. By addressing the full spectrum of patient preferences, needs and values while endorsing collaboration among healthcare professionals, this system strives to improve health outcomes, enhance patient satisfaction, and create a more efficient and effective healthcare delivery model.

4.4 OPERATIONAL MEASURES OF THE AMERICAN HEALTHCARE DELIVERY SYSTEM

The American healthcare delivery system is a complex network characterized by a multitude of operational measures designed to enhance quality, safety, efficiency, and a positive patient experience. (Niles, 2024, Shi et al., 2014).

One critical operational measure is the implementation of electronic health records (EHRs), which facilitate the seamless sharing of patient information across different healthcare providers. EHRs strive to improve coordination of care, reduce service errors, and ensure that patients receive appropriate treatments at the right time, in the right amount, and to the right person. Additionally, the adoption of health information exchanges (HIEs) enables broader data interoperability, further enhancing the continuity of care across various healthcare settings (Pai et al., 2022).

Another critical operational measure is the emphasis on performance metrics and quality improvement initiatives (Chow-Chua et al., 2002). Healthcare providers are increasingly using data-driven approaches to monitor and improve clinical outcomes. This involves the use of standardized performance indicators, such as hospital readmission rates, infection rates, and patient mortality rates, to identify areas needing improvement and to implement targeted interventions. Continuous quality improvement programs, often supported by federal and state initiatives, encourage healthcare organizations to strive for excellence in patient care through regular assessment and refinement of clinical practices to best-in-class achievement.

Operational efficiency in the American healthcare delivery system is also driven by the adoption of lean management principles and process optimization strategies (Fiorillo et al., 2021). Healthcare organizations are applying these principles to streamline workflows, reduce waste, and enhance productivity. For example, hospitals are redesigning their emergency department processes to reduce patient wait times and improve throughput. Similarly, the use of telehealth services has expanded, offering patients convenient access to care while alleviating the burden on physical healthcare facilities. These operational enhancements contribute to a more responsive and efficient healthcare delivery system.

Financial management and cost containment are crucial operational measures within the American healthcare delivery system (Stadhouders et al., 2019). This includes implementing value-based payment models, such as accountable care organizations (ACOs) and bundled payment arrangements, which incentivize providers to deliver high-quality care while controlling costs. By shifting from fee-for-service to value-based models of care, healthcare providers are encouraged to focus on health prevention and promotion, reduce unnecessary procedures, and enhance patient outcomes. Additionally, rigorous financial oversight and strategic resource allocation help healthcare organizations maintain financial stability and invest in innovations that further improve care delivery.

Finally, workforce development and management are vital operational measures in the American healthcare delivery system (Pittman et al., 2016). Ensuring an adequate supply of skilled healthcare professionals, including physicians, nurses, and allied health workers, is essential for maintaining high standards of patient care. This involves strategic recruitment, retention initiatives, and ongoing professional development programs to equip healthcare workers with the latest knowledge, hard skills, and soft skills. Addressing workforce challenges, such as burnout and staff shortages, through supportive policies and flexible work arrangements, is also crucial for sustaining a resilient and effective healthcare delivery system.

4.5 A CLOSER LOOK AT THE OPERATIONAL MEASURES OF THE AMERICAN HEALTHCARE DELIVERY SYSTEM

Delving deeper into the operational measures of the American healthcare delivery system reveals a complex array of metrics aimed at evaluating efficiency, quality, accessibility, and patient outcomes. Foundational performance indicators include patient reported outcome measures, readmission rates, hospital-acquired infection rates, and average length of stay. The system also scrutinizes cost-related measures, such as healthcare expenditure per capita and the financial performance of healthcare institutions, e.g., revenue cycle management. Moreover, fidelity to evidence-based clinical practice guidelines and the implementation of health information systems and technology are critical components that enhance coordination and streamline processes. By continuously monitoring and analyzing these operational measures, healthcare stakeholders can identify areas for improvement, implement targeted interventions, and ultimately strive towards a more efficient and patient-centered healthcare delivery system.

The quality and safety of patient care are paramount in healthcare, focusing on delivering high standards of treatment while minimizing risks and harm to patients. This encompasses a range of practices including empirically-derived evidence-based medicine, continuous staff education, and adherence to stringent clinical guidelines. Safety protocols such as infection control, medication management, and the use of technology to monitor patient health are crucial. Moreover, fostering a culture of transparency and accountability, where healthcare professionals feel empowered to report errors without fear of reprisal, significantly contributes to improving patient outcomes and preventing adverse events.

Access to healthcare services involves ensuring that individuals can obtain the medical care they need in a timely manner. This includes removing barriers such as geographical location, financial constraints, and social determinants of health. Effective navigation systems are essential, guiding patients through complex healthcare networks and ensuring they reach the appropriate services needed promptly. This can involve the use of patient navigators, digital health e-platforms, and integrated care models that streamline referrals and coordinate care among multiple providers. Improving access and navigation helps reduce disparities in healthcare and enhances overall health outcomes.

Managing the total cost of care involves monitoring and controlling healthcare expenses while ensuring that patients receive necessary and appropriate services. Utilization management plays a critical role in this process by evaluating the medical necessity, appropriateness, and efficiency of healthcare services. This includes pre-authorization for high-cost procedures, concurrent review of ongoing treatments, and retrospective analysis of completed care. Effective utilization management helps avoid unnecessary procedures, reduces waste, and ensures that resources are allocated efficiently and effectively. Balancing cost control with high-quality patient care is essential to achieving value-based sustainable healthcare systems.

Patient-reported outcome measures (PROMs) and the patient experience are vital components of assessing healthcare quality from the patient's perspective. PROMs involve collecting data directly from patients about their health status, quality of life, and functional outcomes following medical treatments. This information is critical for understanding the impact of healthcare interventions and for tailoring care to the patient's preferences, needs, and values. Additionally, patient experience surveys capture feedback on various aspects of care, including communication with providers, ease of access to services, and overall satisfaction e.g., would you refer a close friend or family member to your current provider? Focusing on these measures helps healthcare providers identify areas for improvement, foster patient-centered care, and enhance the overall patient experience.

4.6 QUANTIFICATION OF UNINTENDED CONSEQUENCES OF HEALTHCARE DELIVERY

The unintended consequences of healthcare delivery are an important area of study as they can significantly impact patient outcomes, healthcare costs, and system efficiency (Berry et al., 2022; Norton et al., 2020; Rahman et al., 2020).

One common unintended consequence is medical errors, which can occur due to miscommunication, misdiagnosis, or procedural mistakes. Quantifying medical errors involves analyzing data from incident reports, patient records, and malpractice claims. Studies estimate that medical errors are the third leading cause of death in the US (Ahmad et al., 2021), highlighting the critical need for robust systems to track and mitigate these errors. By using metrics such as error rates, patient harm incidents, and associated costs, healthcare organizations can better understand the prevalence and impact of medical errors and implement strategies to reduce them (Vahidi et al., 2020).

Another significant unintended consequence is the issue of healthcare-associated infections (HAIs). These infections can occur in various healthcare settings, including hospitals and long-term care facilities, and can lead to severe patient outcomes and increased healthcare costs. Quantification of HAIs involves tracking infection rates through surveillance systems, analyzing patient data, and monitoring the effectiveness of infection control measures. Metrics such as the rate of specific infections per 1,000 patient days and the cost of treatment for these infections provide valuable insights. By quantifying HAIs, healthcare organizations can identify high-risk areas, implement targeted interventions, and monitor the effectiveness of infection prevention strategies (Haque et al., 2020).

The overuse, underuse, or misuse of diagnostics and treatments is another unintended consequence that can be quantified (Mekonnen et al., 2020). This includes unnecessary diagnostic tests, inappropriate prescribing of medications, and inappropriate treatment of acute and chronic conditions, all of which can lead to patient harm and increased costs. Quantifying inappropriate use involves analyzing healthcare utilization data, reviewing patient records, and comparing practices against established best-in-class clinical practice guidelines. Metrics such as the frequency of specific tests or treatments per patient population and the associated costs of inappropriate use provide a clear picture of the extent of the problem. By identifying patterns of inappropriateness, healthcare providers can look to evidence-based practices, improve patient safety, and reduce unnecessary healthcare spending.

The quantification of patient readmissions is also crucial in understanding unintended consequences (Becker et al., 2021). Readmissions often indicate inadequate initial treatment or poor post-discharge care and can be costly for both patients and healthcare systems. Tracking readmission rates, especially for conditions like heart failure, pneumonia, and chronic obstructive pulmonary disease (COPD), can highlight gaps in transitions of care and post-discharge support. Metrics such as the 30-day readmission rate and the cost of readmissions help quantify this issue. By analyzing these metrics, healthcare providers can implement interventions such as improved discharge planning, patient and caregiver education, and follow-up care to reduce readmissions and enhance patient outcomes.

Finally, the impact of healthcare delivery on mental health is an unintended consequence that warrants quantification. The stress and emotional toll on both patients and healthcare providers can lead to increasing manifestations of the diseases of despair including depression, anxiety, and suicide. Quantifying this impact involves surveys, interviews, and the use of validated tools to measure mental health outcomes. Metrics such as the prevalence of burnout among healthcare workers, patient satisfaction scores, and the incidence and prevalence of mental health issues provide valuable insights. Understanding these consequences enables healthcare organizations to develop support systems, improve working conditions, and promote mental health and well-being for both patients and staff (Coombs et al., 2021).

Quantifying the unintended consequences of healthcare delivery involves identifying key performance indicators (KPIs) in areas such as medical errors, healthcare-associated infections, overuse of medical interventions, patient readmissions, and mental health impacts. By asking the right questions to obtain appropriate KPI data and then, analyzing the data that is available, healthcare organizations can gain a comprehensive understanding of all of their KPIs, implement targeted interventions, and ultimately improve the quality and safety of healthcare delivery.

4.7 HEALTHCARE STEWARDSHIP AND THE AMERICAN HEALTHCARE DELIVERY SYSTEM

Healthcare stewardship is critically important today due to several pressing challenges and evolving dynamics within America's healthcare delivery systems. These challenges necessitate a focused and culturally responsible approach to managing limited healthcare resources to ensure that the *system* remains effective, efficient, equitable, and sustainable.

Escalating healthcare expenses driven by advanced medical technologies, aging populations, and increasing prevalence of chronic diseases are behind the rising costs of healthcare. Effective stewardship is essential to equitably control the total costs of care including fraud, waste and abuse while maintaining high-quality and safe medical care with positive patient and provider experiences towards the Quintuple Aim. Without careful resource management, rising costs can strain public and private healthcare financing, leading to potential cuts in services or increased financial burden on patients, their families, and the communities in which they live, play and work.

An aging population will undoubtably increase demand for healthcare services. Older adults typically require more medical care, including long-term care and management of chronic conditions. Stewardship ensures that resources are allocated equitably and efficiently to meet the growing demands of an aging population. In addition, the elderly often have multiple comorbidities, requiring holistic, integrated, comprehensive and coordinated care. Effective stewardship helps by using the principles and practices of health systems science in designing open, complex, and adaptive healthcare systems that can manage these complexities.

Non-communicable chronic diseases such as diabetes, cardiovascular disease, chronic obstructive pulmonary disease, neurodegenerative disorders and cancer are becoming more prevalent across-the world. Healthcare stewardship focuses on applying the principles and practices of P^4 Health (health prevention, protection, promotion, and preparedness) and the effective care management of chronic diseases to produce positive health and optimize wellness and wellbeing and reduce total costs of care. The rising rates of obesity, inadequate nutrition, unwholesome dietary intake, lack of physical activity, poor quality sleep, and overwhelming stress all contribute to the incidence and prevalence of chronic diseases. Stewardship promotes essential public health services and initiatives using public health science (i.e., disease surveillance and epidemiology) to address these unhealthy lifestyles and behavioral factors.

Health Inequities and significant disparities exist in healthcare access, navigation, quality and the patient experience across different socio-economic, racial, and geographic groups. Stewardship aims to address these inequities by ensuring equitable distribution of resources and targeted interventions for underserved and vulnerable populations. Effective stewardship involves addressing the negative social determinants of health such as inequitable access to a comprehensive positive educational experience, inadequate and safe housing, food insecurity, and a lack of reliable transportation, can have a profound impact on positive health outcomes.

Rapid advancements in medical technology, big data analytics, interoperability and digital health tools offer opportunities for improving medical care but also require careful management to ensure they are used securely, effectively and equitably. Leveraging health data and analytics to inform healthy public policies and practices is a critical aspect of stewardship, enabling more precise and effective healthcare interventions.

Environmental and Public Health Challenges including Anthropogenic climate changes are impacting health in various ways, from increasing the prevalence of communicable (e.g., emerging infectious diseases) and non-communicable diseases (e.g., diabetes, hypertension) to exacerbating health disparities. Stewardship includes preparing healthcare systems to address these impacts. The SARS CoV-2 viral (i.e., COVID-19) pandemic highlighted the need for robust stewardship to manage resources, coordinate responses, and ensure public health preparedness. The Public Health Exposome is a framework designed to track exposures throughout a person's life to understand their impact on health span. It aims to integrate the complex relationships between an individual's environmental exposures, personal health, the environment, and population-level disparities. The exposome includes both endogenous and exogenous exposures, such as diet, lifestyle, genetics, physiology, epigenetics, and environmental and occupational factors. The exposome represents the environmental, non-genetic drivers of health and disease, as the etiology of a health condition is rarely explained by a single exposure.

Ensuring that healthcare systems prioritize patient needs, rights, and preferences is a fundamental aspect of stewardship. Making informed and ethical decisions about resource allocation, especially in times of scarcity, is crucial for maintaining trust and fairness in the healthcare system.

In an increasingly globalized world, health issues transcend national borders. Effective stewardship involves international cooperation, collaboration and coordination and the sharing of best clinical and non-clinical practices to tackle global health challenges. Healthcare stewardship aligns with the United Nation's Agenda for Sustainable Development (2015), especially the sustainable development goals focused on health, wellness, and well-being.

Healthcare stewardship is essential today to navigate the complexities and challenges of modern healthcare systems. By promoting efficiency, equity, quality, and sustainability, effective stewardship helps ensure that healthcare systems can meet current and future health needs, improve health outcomes, and maintain public trust. The role of stewardship is to balance the various demands on the healthcare system while fostering innovation and resilience in the face of evolving health challenges.

4.8 HEALTHCARE STEWARDSHIP AND THE AMERICAN MEDICAL SUPPLY CHAIN

The medical supply chain is a critical component of healthcare stewardship, ensuring that medical supplies and equipment are available where and when they are needed while minimizing waste and inefficiencies. Efficient supply chain management involves the careful planning, procurement, storage, and distribution of medical products. By leveraging advanced technologies and data analytics, healthcare organizations can forecast demand more accurately, reducing the risk of overstocking or stockouts. This precision in inventory management not only optimizes resource use but also ensures that healthcare providers have access to essential supplies, enhancing patient care and safety (Ziat et al., 2020; Blanchard, 2021)

Additionally, the medical supply chain plays a pivotal role in cost containment, a key aspect of healthcare stewardship (Ketokivi et al., 2020). By negotiating better prices with suppliers, adopting group purchasing strategies, and implementing value-based procurement practices, healthcare organizations can significantly reduce their expenditure on medical supplies. This cost savings can be redirected toward other critical areas of patient care and facility improvement. Moreover, efficient supply chain operations can reduce operational costs related to storage, transportation, and handling of supplies, contributing to the overall financial sustainability of healthcare institutions.

Sustainability is another crucial area where the medical supply chain impacts healthcare stewardship (AlJaberi et al., 2020; Zhu et al., 2020). By incorporating environmentally friendly practices, such as reducing packaging waste, choosing sustainable materials, and implementing recycling programs, healthcare organizations can lessen their environmental footprint. Sustainable supply chain practices not only benefit the environment but also resonate with the growing emphasis on corporate social responsibility in the healthcare sector. This alignment with sustainability goals can enhance the reputation of healthcare institutions and contribute to broader public health objectives.

Furthermore, the resilience and agility of the medical supply chain are vital for effective healthcare stewardship, especially during crises such as pandemics or natural disasters (Rehman et al., 2022). A well-prepared and flexible supply chain can quickly adapt to sudden changes in demand, ensuring the continuous availability of critical medical supplies. This resilience is achieved through strategic stockpiling, diversifying suppliers, and utilizing robust logistics networks. By maintaining a reliable supply chain, healthcare organizations can provide uninterrupted care, prevent shortages of essential items, and support public health preparedness for and responses during emergencies (Patel et al., 2022)

Lastly, the medical supply chain contributes to healthcare stewardship through the adoption of innovative technologies and practices (Yang et al., 2021). Implementing automated inventory systems, utilizing blockchain for enhanced transparency and traceability, and employing artificial intelligence for predictive analytics are just a few examples of how technology can optimize supply chain operations. These innovations lead to greater efficiency, reduced errors, and improved decision-making, ultimately enhancing the quality of care provided to patients. By staying at the forefront of technological advancements, the medical supply chain can continuously improve and support the overarching goals of healthcare stewardship (Blanchard, 2021, Khan et al., 2021)

4.9 THE US MEDICAL-INDUSTRIAL COMPLEX AND THE US MEDICAL SUPPLY CHAIN

The U.S. medical-industrial complex refers to the network of private and public organizations involved in the production and distribution of healthcare services, medical equipment, pharmaceuticals, and related technologies (Rutkove et al., 2016). This complex encompasses hospitals, insurance companies, pharmaceutical manufacturers, medical device producers, research institutions, and regulatory bodies. The system is characterized by its significant integration of profit-driven motives with healthcare delivery, leading to a complex interplay between market forces and public health needs. This structure has led to considerable innovation and advancements in medical technologies and treatments, often pushing the boundaries of what's possible in healthcare.

However, the U.S. medical-industrial complex has also been the subject of extensive criticism and debate. One major point of contention is the high cost of healthcare in the United States, which is largely attributed to the profit-oriented nature of the industry (Salmon et al., 2021). Unlike many other developed nations, the U.S. lacks a universal healthcare system, resulting in significant disparities in access to care. The emphasis on profit can sometimes prioritize expensive treatments and procedures over more cost-effective, proactive care approaches. Additionally, the relationship between pharmaceutical companies and regulatory bodies has raised concerns about the potential for conflicts of interest, particularly when it comes to drug pricing and the approval of new medications.

Moreover, the insurance industry plays a pivotal role in shaping the medical-industrial complex (Browner et al., 2019). The complex billing systems, negotiations over service prices, and the exclusion of certain treatments or medications from coverage plans are all influenced by the profit-driven motives of insurance providers. This often leaves patients with high out-of-pocket costs, even when they have insurance. The complexity and opacity of pricing within the system can also lead to unexpected and exorbitant medical bills, contributing to medical debt, which is a leading cause of bankruptcy in the U.S.

The U.S. medical-industrial complex also impacts the research and development sector (Blume, 2020). While the pursuit of new medical technologies and drugs is crucial for advancing healthcare, the heavy reliance on private funding can skew research priorities towards more profitable areas, sometimes at the expense of essential but less lucrative fields, such as vaccines or treatments for rare diseases. The influence of pharmaceutical companies and the prioritization of profits can also lead to issues such as the over-prescription of medications and the promotion of costly new treatments over established, effective, and cheaper alternatives.

The U.S. medical-industrial complex represents a vast and intricate system with both positive and negative aspects. While it has driven significant advancements in medical technology and treatments, it has also contributed to high healthcare costs, disparities in access, and ethical concerns regarding the prioritization of profit over patient welfare. Balancing the benefits of innovation with the need for equitable and affordable healthcare remains a key challenge for policymakers and stakeholders within this complex system.

The medical supply chain is a fundamental component of the medical industrial complex, providing the necessary infrastructure to deliver medical products and technologies from manufacturers to healthcare providers (Wieland, 2021). This chain encompasses various stages, including production, procurement, distribution, and delivery, all of which are integral to the functioning of the healthcare system. The efficiency and reliability of the medical supply chain ensure that hospitals, clinics, and other healthcare facilities have consistent access to essential supplies, such as medications, medical devices, and personal protective equipment. By ensuring the timely and adequate delivery of these supplies, the supply chain supports the continuity of care and the effective treatment of patients.

Within the medical industrial complex, the medical supply chain also drives innovation and advancement (Salmon et al., 2021). Companies within the medical supply chain invest heavily in research and development to create new medical products and improve existing ones. This innovation leads to the development of cutting-edge technologies and treatments that enhance patient outcomes and contribute to the overall progress of medical science. The competitive nature of the medical supply chain fosters a continuous cycle of improvement and adaptation, ensuring that the healthcare system benefits from the latest advancements and maintains high standards of care.

The economic impact of the medical supply chain within the medical industrial complex is significant (Salmon, 2022). It is a major driver of economic activity, supporting a vast network of manufacturers, suppliers, distributors, and logistics providers. This network creates jobs and stimulates economic growth, contributing to the financial stability of the healthcare sector and the broader economy. Furthermore, the medical supply chain's ability to negotiate pricing and manage costs directly influences the affordability of healthcare services. By optimizing procurement processes and reducing medical waste, the medical supply chain helps to control healthcare costs, making treatments more accessible to patients and improving the overall efficiency of the healthcare system.

Moreover, the medical supply chain plays a critical role in global health by facilitating the distribution of medical products across borders (Dent, 2024). In the context of the medical industrial complex, this global reach is essential for addressing health disparities and ensuring that medical innovations are available to populations worldwide. Through international partnerships and collaborations, the medical supply chain supports global health initiatives, such as vaccination campaigns and disease eradication efforts. By enabling the global exchange of medical goods and knowledge, the supply chain contributes to the improvement of health outcomes on a global scale.

Finally, the medical supply chain is pivotal in ensuring preparedness and resilience within the medical industrial complex (Nguyen, 2023). The ability to respond swiftly to public health emergencies, such as pandemics or natural disasters, relies heavily on a robust and agile supply chain. Strategic stockpiling, diversified sourcing, and advanced logistics capabilities are essential for maintaining the flow of critical medical supplies during crises. By strengthening the resilience of the medical supply chain, the medical-industrial complex can better withstand disruptions and continue to provide essential services, safeguarding public health and ensuring that healthcare systems remain functional under stress.

4.10 REFERENCES

Ahmad, F. B., Anderson, R. N. (2021) The leading causes of death in the US for 2020.*JAMA* 325 (18), 1829-1830.

AlJaberi, O. A., Hussain, M., Drake, P. R. (2020) A framework for measuring sustainability in healthcare systems.*International Journal of Healthcare Management.*

Becker, C., Zumbrunn, S., Beck, K., et al. (2021) Interventions to improve communication at hospital discharge and rates of readmission: a systematic review and meta-analysis.*JAMA Network Open*4 (8): e2119346-e2119346.

Berry, L. L., Attai, D. J., Scammon, D. L., et al. (2022) When the aims and the ends of health care misalign.*Journal of Service Research*25 (1), 160-184.

Blanchard, D. (2021)*Supply chain management best practices.* John Wiley& Sons.

Blume, S. (2020) Medicine, technology and industry. *In*Medicine in the Twentieth Century(pp. 171-185). Taylor& Francis.

Browner, C. H. (2019) Moving beyond Neoliberal Models of Health Care.*Medical Anthropology* 38 (5): 455-458.

Coombs, N. C., Meriwether, W. E., Caringi, J., et al. (2021) Barriers to healthcare access among US adults with mental health challenges: A population-based study.*SSM-PopulationHealth*15:100847.

Chow-Chua, C., Goh, M. (2002) Framework for evaluating performance and quality improvement in hospitals.*Managing Service Quality: An International Journal*12 (1), 54-66.

Dent, M. (2024) The role of the medical–industrial complex in the National Health Services. *In*National Health Services of Western Europe(pp. 285-302). Routledge.

Fiorillo, A., Sorrentino, A., Scala, A., et al. (2021) Improving performance of the hospitalization process by applying the principles of Lean Thinking.*The TQM Journal* 33 (7), 253-271.

Haque, M., McKimm, J., Sartelli, M., et al. (2020) Strategies to prevent healthcare-associated infections: a narrative overview.*Risk Management and Healthcare Policy* 13: 1765-1780.

Health at a Glance 2023: OECD Indicators.(2023).France:OECD Publishing.

Ketokivi, M.,& Mahoney, J. T. (2020) Transaction cost economics as a theory of supply chain efficiency.*Production and Operations Management*29 (4): 1011-1031.

Khan, S. A. R., Godil, D. I., Jabbour, et al. (2021) Green data analytics, blockchain technology for sustainable development, and sustainable supply chain practices: evidence from small and medium enterprises.*Annals of Operations Research* pp 1-25.

Mekonnen, A. B., Redley, B., de Courten, B., et al. (2021) Potentially inappropriate prescribing and its associations with health-related and system-related outcomes in hospitalized older adults: a systematic review and meta-analysis.*British Journal of Clinical Pharmacology*87 (11): 4150-4172.

Niles, N. J. (2023).*Basics of the US health care system*. Burlington, MA: Jones& Bartlett Learning.

Norton, W. E., Chambers, D. A. (2020) Unpacking the complexities of de-implementing inappropriate health interventions. *Implementation Science* 15 (1), 2.

Nguyen, T. (2023)*Building health system resilience*. The Norwegian Defense Research Establishment.

Pai, D. R., Rajan, B., Chakraborty, S. (2022) Do EHR and HIE deliver on their promise? Analysis of Pennsylvania acute care hospitals. *International Journal of Production Economics*245: 108398.

Patel, B. S., Sambasivan, M. (2022) A systematic review of the literature on supply chain agility.*Management Research Review* 45 (2): 236-260.

Pittman, P., Scully-Russ, E. (2016) Workforce planning and development in times of delivery system transformation.*Human Resources for Health* 14: 1-15.

Rahman, M., Meyers, D. J., Wright, B. (2020) Unintended consequences of observation stay use may disproportionately burden Medicare beneficiaries in disadvantaged neighborhoods. *Mayo Clinic Proceedings*95 (12): 2589-2592.

Rehman, O. U., Ali, Y. (2022) Enhancing healthcare supply chain resilience: decision-making in a fuzzy environment.*The International Journal of Logistics Management* 33 (2): 520-546.

Rutkove, S. B.,& Rutkove, S. B. (2016) Working with Industry. *Biomedical Research: An Insider's Guide*, 241-245.

Salmon, J. W. (2022) Organizing medical care for profit. *In*Issues in the political economy of health care(pp. 143-186). Routledge.

Salmon, J. W., Thompson, S. L., Salmon, J. W., et al. (2021) History of the Corporatization of American Medicine: The Market Paradigm Reigns.*The Corporatization of American Health Care: The Rise of Corporate Hegemony and the Loss of Professional Autonomy* pp 1-59.

Shi, L.,& Singh, D. A. (2014).*Delivering health care in America: A systems approach*. Sunbury, MA: Jones& Bartlett Learning.

Stadhouders, N., Kruse, F., Tanke, M., et al. (2019) Effective healthcare cost-containment policies: a systematic review.*Health Policy* 123 (1), 71-79.

UN General Assembly. (2015)*Transforming our world: the 2030 Agenda for Sustainable Development.*

Vahidi, S., Mirhashemi, S. H., Noorbakhsh, M., et al. (2020). Clinical errors: Implementing root cause analysis in an area health service. *International Journal of Healthcare Management* 13: 1-12.

Wieland, A. (2021) Dancing the supply chain: Toward transformative supply chain management. *Journal of Supply Chain Management.* 57 (1), 58-73.

Yang, M., Fu, M., Zhang, Z. (2021) The adoption of digital technologies in supply chains: Drivers, process and impact. *Technological Forecasting and Social Change* 169: 120795.

Zhu, G., Chou, M. C., Tsai, C. W. (2020) Lessons learned from the COVID-19 pandemic exposing the shortcomings of current supply chain operations: A long-term prescriptive offering. *Sustainability* 12 (14): 5858.

Ziat, A., Sefiani, N., Reklaoui, K., et al. (2020) A generic framework for hospital supply chain. *International Journal of Healthcare Management.*

CHAPTER 5

HEALTHCARE STEWARDSHIP AND HEALTH SYSTEMS SCIENCE

5.1 FOUNDATIONAL ELEMENTS OF HEALTH SYSTEMS SCIENCE

Health Systems Science (HSS) is an emerging field that provides a comprehensive framework for understanding and improving healthcare delivery (Skochelak et al., 2021). It is defined as the study of health systems and how they promote health in real-world settings.It is also a framework for understanding how medical care is delivered, how health professionals work collaboratively, and how the health system can improve patient care.HSS also explores how human relationships influence the production of positive health and optimize wellness and well-being, such as when a care team works together to solve a problem or a community tries to overcome biases.

Health Systems Science encompasses the foundational elements necessary to navigate and enhance adaptive and complex health systems effectively. These elements include healthcare policy and economics, clinical informatics and health technology, population health, value-based care, and health systems improvement. Together, these components create a holistic, integrated, and comprehensive approach to healthcare that emphasizes efficiency, effectiveness, and equity.

Healthcare policy and economics are critical foundational elements of Health Systems Science. Understanding the intricacies of healthcare policies, regulations, and economic factors is essential for shaping effective healthcare systems. This involves analyzing how policies impact patient care, healthcare costs, and access to services. By understanding the economic principles that govern healthcare financing and reimbursement, healthcare professionals can advocate for policies that promote sustainability and equity in healthcare delivery. This knowledge is crucial for designing and implementing systems that are financially viable and capable of providing high-quality care to diverse populations.

Clinical informatics and health technology play a pivotal role in modern health systems. The integration of electronic health records (EHRs), telemedicine, and data analytics into clinical practice enhances the efficiency and quality of care. Health Systems Science emphasizes the importance of leveraging technology to improve patient outcomes, streamline workflows, and support decision-making. Clinical informatics enables healthcare providers to access real-time patient data, track health trends, and implement evidence-based practices. Additionally, advancements in health technology, such as artificial intelligence and machine learning, offer new opportunities for predictive analytics and personalized medicine.

Population health is another key component of Health Systems Science. This element focuses on improving health outcomes for entire populations by addressing social determinants of health, promoting proactive care, and managing chronic diseases. Population health strategies involve community-based interventions, health education, and healthy public policies that reduce health disparities. By adopting a population health management strategy, healthcare systems can identify at-risk groups, implement targeted interventions, and measure the impact of these efforts on community health. This holistic view of health considers the broader social, economic, and environmental factors that influence well-being, ensuring that healthcare systems address the root causes of poor health.

Value-based care is central to the principles of Health Systems Science. This approach prioritizes patient outcomes and cost-effectiveness over the volume of services provided. Value-based models of care, such as accountable care organizations (ACOs) and bundled payment programs, incentivize healthcare providers to deliver high-quality, holistic, integrated, comprehensive, and coordinated care. By focusing on value rather than volume, healthcare systems can improve the overall patient experience, reduce unnecessary procedures, and lower healthcare costs. This shift towards value-based models of care requires a deep understanding of quality improvement science, patient-centered care, and collaborative practice among healthcare professionals.

Health systems improvement is a continuous process that involves assessing and enhancing the performance of healthcare systems. This element of Health Systems Science emphasizes the use of quality improvement methodologies, such as Plan-Do-Study-Act (PDSA) cycles, Lean, and Six Sigma, to identify inefficiencies and implement solutions. Continuous improvement efforts focus on enhancing patient safety, reducing medical errors, and optimizing clinical workflows. By fostering a culture of creativity, innovation, and accountability, healthcare systems can adapt to the changing needs of their communities and improve the overall quality of care.

In summary, Health Systems Science provides a comprehensive framework that integrates healthcare policy and economics, clinical informatics and health technology, population health, value-based care, and health systems improvement. These foundational elements are essential for understanding and enhancing the complex healthcare landscape. By adopting the principles of Health Systems Science, healthcare professionals can create more efficient, effective, and equitable healthcare systems that meet the needs of diverse populations and adapt to emerging challenges.

5.2 THE IMPACT OF HEALTHCARE STEWARDSHIP ON HEALTH SYSTEMS SCIENCE

Healthcare stewardship significantly impacts health systems science, which is the study of how healthcare is delivered, how healthcare professionals work together, and how the healthcare system can improve patient outcomes (Skochelak et aal., 2021). This interdisciplinary field encompasses various aspects of healthcare, including policy, management, economics, and patient care. Effective stewardship influences health systems science in several key ways.

Healthcare stewardship's emphasis on resource optimization directly impacts health systems science by promoting efficient use of financial, human, and material resources. By applying principles of stewardship, health systems can reduce waste, streamline operations, and implement evidence-based practices that enhance patient care. This focus on efficiency leads to the development and application of methodologies within health systems science that improve resource allocation and operational effectiveness. Researchers and practitioners in this field can use big data analytics, computational science, and bio-informatics to identify inefficiencies, monitor performance, and implement strategies that ensure the best use of resources, ultimately leading to improved health outcomes and system sustainability.

The principle of equity and accessibility in healthcare stewardship significantly shapes health systems science by highlighting the importance of addressing disparities in healthcare access and navigation. Health systems science explores how to design and implement healthcare delivery models of care that ensure all individuals, regardless of their socioeconomic status or geographic location, have access to necessary medical care. Stewardship-driven healthy public policies and initiatives, such as expanding government-sponsored insurance coverage and enhancing primary care services in underserved areas, provide valuable case studies and frameworks for researchers and practitioners. These efforts inform the development of equitable healthcare models of care that promote inclusivity and reduce health disparities, which are central themes in health systems science.

Healthcare stewardship's focus on accountability and transparency influences health systems science by driving quality improvement science and patient safety initiatives ensuring that healthcare providers are held accountable for their performance. Health systems science examines how healthcare organizations can implement quality improvement processes, such as clinical guidelines, key performance indicators, and patient safety protocols to enhance healthcare delivery. Stewardship principles encourage continuous monitoring and evaluation of healthcare practices, fostering a culture of accountability and excellence. This alignment with health systems science promotes the development of robust frameworks for quality assurance and performance improvement, leading to higher standards of care and better patient outcomes.

The sustainability principle in healthcare stewardship impacts health systems science by emphasizing the importance of capacity-building, long-term planning and the prudent use of resources. Health systems science explores strategies to create open, complex, integrated, resilient and adaptable healthcare systems that can withstand future challenges, such as major demographic shifts, technological advancements, and emerging health threats. By incorporating sustainability into their research and practice, health systems scientists can develop innovative models for proactive care, chronic disease management, and environmentally-friendly healthcare practices. This focus ensures that healthcare systems remain viable and effective over the long term, aligning with the goals of both stewardship and health systems science.

Healthcare stewardship's commitment to ethical considerations and collaboration enhances the study of health systems science by promoting ethical decision-making and fostering partnerships among stakeholders. Health systems science examines how ethical frameworks can guide resource allocation, patient-centered care, and healthy public policy development. Stewardship principles ensure that decisions are made transparently and inclusively, respecting patient preferences, needs and values, and promoting fairness. Additionally, the collaborative nature of stewardship encourages partnerships between government agencies, healthcare providers, patients, and communities. These collaborations are crucial for addressing complex health challenges and developing comprehensive solutions, which are critical areas of focus in health systems science.

Healthcare stewardship profoundly impacts health systems science by influencing how resources are managed, promoting equity and access, driving quality improvement, ensuring sustainability, and fostering ethical and collaborative approaches. These principles guide the development of more efficient, equitable, and resilient healthcare systems, ultimately improving patient outcomes and advancing the field of health systems science.

5.3 HEALTHCARE STEWARDSHIP'S IMPACT ON POPULATION HEALTH MANAGEMENT

Population health management (PHM) is a comprehensive approach to improving the health outcomes of a group by monitoring and identifying individual patients within that group (Krieger, 2024; van Vooren et al., 2020)

One essential function of PHM is the collection and analysis of health data. This involves gathering detailed information on patient demographics, health behaviors, disease prevalence, and healthcare utilization. Advanced data analytics are then used to identify trends, risk factors, and health disparities within a defined cohort of the population. By understanding these patterns, healthcare providers can design targeted interventions aimed at reducing the incidence of chronic diseases, improving overall health outcomes, producing positive health, and optimizing wellness and well-being.

Another crucial function of PHM is the implementation of coordinated care strategies. This includes developing transitions of care that address the specific needs of individuals, particularly those with chronic conditions or complex healthcare needs. Coordinated care ensures that patients receive timely and appropriate medical services, reducing the likelihood of hospital readmissions and emergency room visits. This approach often involves multidisciplinary teams, including primary care physicians, specialists, nurses, and social workers, working collaboratively to provide holistic, integrated, comprehensive, and continuous care. Effective coordination of care enhances patient satisfaction, improves health outcomes, and optimizes resource use.

Patient engagement and education are also vital components of PHM. Empowering individuals to take an active role in their health management leads to self-efficacy, self-actualization, self-management, and better health behaviors and outcomes. This can be achieved through health coaching, educational programs, and the use of digital health tools such as patient portals and mobile SMART apps. These resources provide patients with access to their health information, personalized health tips, and reminders for health prevention screening services. Engaged and informed patients are more likely to follow personalized treatment plans, regularly attend age-specific wellness check-ups, and adopt healthier lifestyles. These actions significantly enhance the overall effectiveness of Population Health Management (PHM).

Proactive care and early intervention are foundational to solid population health management. By focusing on health prevention, PHM aims to reduce the burden of disease before it becomes more severe and costly to treat. This includes comprehensive wellness examinations, vaccinations, and risk factor identification for chronic conditions. Lifestyle and behavioral modification programs using neurobiology of change are designed to mitigate risk factors for chronic conditions such as diabetes, heart disease, and cancer. Early intervention strategies, such as managing hypertension before it leads to more serious cardiovascular conditions, are critical in minimizing long-term health complications and mitigating rising healthcare costs. Health prevention, health promotion, and health protection not only improve individual health outcomes but also contribute to the sustainability of the healthcare system by keeping people in a state of wellness rather than a state of disease.

Lastly, PHM emphasizes the importance of social determinants of health (SDOH). These are non-medical factors that influence health outcomes, such as economic stability, education, social and community context, and access to healthcare and nutrition. Addressing SDOH involves collaborating with community organizations, policymakers, and other stakeholders to create supportive environments that promote health equity. Interventions might include programs to improve housing conditions, increase access to nutritious food, and enhance educational opportunities. By tackling these broader determinants of health, PHM can more effectively improve the well-being of populations, particularly vulnerable and underserved groups (Chim et al.)

Implementing Population Health Management (PHM) presents several challenges that healthcare organizations must navigate to achieve success (Omri et al., 2019). One of the primary challenges is data integration and interoperability. Effective PHM relies on the seamless integration of data from various sources, including electronic health records (EHRs), claims data, social determinants of health, and patient-generated data. However, healthcare data is often siloed across different systems and formats, making it difficult to aggregate and analyze comprehensively. Ensuring interoperability between these disparate systems requires significant investment in technology and the development of standardized data exchange protocols, which can be both complex and costly.

Another significant challenge is the need for cultural and organizational change within healthcare institutions. Transitioning to a population health-focused model requires a shift in mindset from treating individual patients to managing the health of entire populations. This change can be met with resistance from healthcare providers who are accustomed to the traditional fee-for-service model. Additionally, fostering a culture of collaboration and care coordination among multidisciplinary teams is essential but can be difficult to achieve. Overcoming these cultural barriers involves continuous education, leadership support, and aligning incentives to promote value-based care.

Financial and resource constraints also pose a substantial obstacle to PHM implementation. Developing and maintaining the infrastructure needed for PHM, such as advanced analytics platforms, patient engagement tools, and care coordination systems, requires significant financial investment. Many healthcare organizations, particularly smaller practices and those serving underserved populations, may struggle to secure the necessary funding. Additionally, recruiting and retaining skilled professionals who can manage and analyze population health data and lead PHM initiatives is a challenge, given the competitive healthcare job market.

Patient engagement is another critical hurdle in PHM implementation. Achieving meaningful patient participation requires overcoming barriers such as health literacy, access to technology, and socio-economic factors that affect individuals' ability to engage with their healthcare. Ensuring that patients understand their health conditions, adhere to treatment plans, and use available health management tools effectively is essential for the success of PHM programs. This necessitates tailored communication strategies and support systems that address the diverse needs of the population.

Lastly, addressing social determinants of health (SDOH) remains a complex and multifaceted challenge. Effective PHM requires identifying and mitigating the impact of SDOH, such as poverty, education, housing, and access to nutritious food, which significantly influence health outcomes. However, healthcare organizations often lack the resources and partnerships necessary to address these broader determinants comprehensively. Building collaborations with community organizations, policymakers, and other stakeholders is crucial but can be difficult to establish and sustain.

In summary, while PHM holds great promise for improving health outcomes and reducing costs, its implementation is fraught with challenges. These include data integration and interoperability issues, cultural and organizational resistance, financial and resource limitations, patient engagement barriers, and the complexity of addressing social determinants of health. Overcoming these challenges requires a concerted effort from all stakeholders involved, including healthcare providers, payers, policymakers, and the community.

Population health management (PHM) significantly influences healthcare stewardship by emphasizing the proactive management of health outcomes for entire populations rather than focusing solely on individual patient care. This approach encourages healthcare providers to consider a broader range of determinants of health, including social, economic, and environmental factors. By addressing these determinants, PHM aims to prevent diseases before they occur, reduce health disparities, and promote overall well-being. This shift from reactive to proactive care leads to more efficient use of healthcare resources, reducing unnecessary hospital admissions, emergency room visits, and redundant testing, thus fostering better stewardship of healthcare resources.

Furthermore, PHM leverages data analytics and health information technology to identify at-risk populations and implement targeted interventions. This data-driven approach enables healthcare systems to allocate resources more effectively, ensuring that interventions are directed where they are most needed. By continuously monitoring population health metrics, healthcare providers can quickly identify trends and respond to emerging health issues, further enhancing resource management. The focus on proactive care and chronic disease management under PHM not only improves patient outcomes but also reduces healthcare costs, supporting sustainable healthcare systems and better stewardship of financial resources.

5.4 HEALTHCARE STEWARDSHIP'S IMPACT ON PEOPLE-CENTERED CARE

People-centered care is an approach to healthcare that prioritizes the needs, preferences, and values of individuals and communities. The foundational elements of people-centered care encompass several key principles and practices that collectively ensure that care is holistic, respectful, and responsive to the needs of patients (WHO, 2015a; WHO, 2015b; WHO, 2018; Santana et al., 2018).

At the core of people-centered care is the respect for each patient's expressed needs, preferences, and values. This involves treating patients with dignity, listening to their concerns, and incorporating their input into care decisions. Respecting patients as individuals means acknowledging their unique circumstances, cultures, and backgrounds, and ensuring that care is tailored to meet their specific needs with humility and empathy.

Effective communication is essential for people-centered care. This involves providing patients with clear, comprehensive, and accessible information about their health, treatment options, and care plans. Transparent communication enables patients to make informed choices about their care using shared-decision making with their provider. It also involves listening actively to patients' questions and concerns, ensuring that they feel heard and understood.

People-centered care requires seamless coordination among healthcare providers and across different levels of the healthcare system. This includes integrating services to provide continuous and comprehensive medical care, including physical, mental, and emotional services, and ensuring that all members of the healthcare team are aligned in their approach to patient care. Collaboration extends to involving patients and their families as active partners in the care process, encouraging shared decision-making.

This approach recognizes that health, wellness, and well-being are influenced by a wide range of factors, including physical, emotional, social, and environmental determinants. Holistic care addresses all these aspects, ensuring that patients receive comprehensive support that goes beyond treating specific medical conditions. This may involve providing mental health services, social support, and addressing social determinants of health that impact patient outcomes.

Ensuring that healthcare is accessible to all individuals, regardless of their socio-economic status, geographic location, or background, is fundamental to people-centered care. This involves reducing barriers to access, such as financial costs, transportation issues, and language barriers. Equity in healthcare ensures that all patients receive fair treatment and that care is provided based on individual needs, preferences, and values, rather than systemic biases or inequalities.

Empowering patients to take an active role in their health and medical care is a critical element of people-centered care. This involves providing education and resources that enable patients to manage their health effectively, encouraging self-efficacy, self-actualization, and self-management, and supporting patients in setting and achieving their health goals. Engagement also means fostering a supportive non-threatening environment where patients feel comfortable discussing their health concerns, needs, preferences, and values.

Delivering care with cultural humility and empathy is essential for building trust and truthfulness with patients. Healthcare providers should strive to understand patients' experiences and emotions, demonstrating genuine care and concern for their health, wellness and well-being. Provider's awareness of the need for cultural humility and empathy helps to create a positive healthcare experience and can significantly impact patient satisfaction and health outcomes.

Recognizing and respecting the diverse cultural backgrounds of patients is crucial in providing people-centered care. Healthcare providers should be trained in cultural competence, enabling them to deliver medical care that is sensitive to cultural differences and responsive to the unique needs of diverse patient populations. This involves understanding cultural beliefs and practices related to health and illness and incorporating this knowledge into care plans.

By integrating these foundational elements, healthcare delivery systems can create an environment that prioritizes the needs, preferences, and values of patients, leading to improved health outcomes, higher patient satisfaction, and more efficient and effective care delivery.

Implementing people-centered care, while beneficial for improving patient outcomes and satisfaction, presents several significant challenges for healthcare organizations. One of the primary hurdles is shifting from a provider-centric to a people-centric approach. This cultural transformation requires healthcare providers and institutions to reorient their practices, policies, and priorities around the needs, preferences, and values of patients. This shift can be met with resistance from healthcare professionals who are accustomed to traditional, provider-driven models of care. Overcoming this challenge requires comprehensive training, leadership support, and continuous education to instill a patient-centered mindset throughout the organization.

Another critical challenge is achieving effective communication and coordination among healthcare teams. People-centered care emphasizes collaboration among multidisciplinary providers, patients, and caregivers to ensure holistic and coordinated care delivery. However, fragmented communication systems, disparate electronic health records (EHRs), and varying levels of healthcare literacy among patients can hinder effective teamwork and information sharing. Achieving seamless integration and communication across different healthcare settings and specialties requires robust technological infrastructure and standardized protocols, which can be costly and complex to implement.

Ensuring equitable access to people-centered care is another significant challenge. Disparities in healthcare access based on socio-economic status, geographic location, language, and cultural background can prevent some individuals from benefiting fully from patient-centered initiatives. Overcoming these barriers involves addressing social determinants of health, improving health literacy, and implementing healthy public policies that promote inclusivity and equity in healthcare delivery. Healthcare organizations must develop strategies to reach underserved populations and ensure that all patients have equal opportunities to participate in and benefit from people-centered care initiatives.

Measuring and demonstrating the impact of people-centered care presents additional challenges. Unlike traditional metrics focused on clinical outcomes and cost-effectiveness, evaluating people-centered outcomes such as satisfaction, empowerment, and quality of life requires innovative measurement tools and methodologies. Healthcare organizations must develop robust evaluation frameworks that capture the multidimensional benefits of people-centered care while ensuring accountability and transparency in reporting outcomes to stakeholders.

Lastly, sustaining a commitment to people-centered care amidst evolving healthcare policies, financial pressures, and competing priorities poses ongoing challenges. Implementing and maintaining people-centered initiatives require long-term investment in resources, infrastructure, and workforce development. Healthcare leaders must advocate for policies that support people-centered care and demonstrate the value of these initiatives in terms of improved health outcomes, reduced healthcare costs, and enhanced patient experience. By addressing these challenges systematically and collaboratively, healthcare organizations can successfully implement and sustain people-centered care models that prioritize the well-being and satisfaction of patients.

People-centered care profoundly impacts healthcare stewardship by prioritizing the needs, preferences, and values of patients in all aspects of care delivery. This approach fosters a holistic view of health that goes beyond treating illnesses to considering patients' overall health, wellness, and well-being, including their physical, emotional, and social needs. By involving patients in shared decision-making and tailoring care plans to their unique circumstances, healthcare providers can enhance the patient experience, patient satisfaction, adherence to treatment plans, and health outcomes. This personalized care reduces the likelihood of unnecessary procedures and hospital readmissions, promoting more efficient use of healthcare resources and contributing to better stewardship.

Moreover, people-centered care encourages the integration of services across the healthcare continuum, ensuring that patients receive coordinated and continuous care. This integration minimizes fragmented care, reduces duplication of services, and prevents gaps in treatment, which are often costly and inefficient. By fostering strong communication and collaboration among healthcare providers, people-centered care supports a more seamless and effective healthcare delivery system. This holistic and coordinated approach not only improves patient experiences and outcomes but also optimizes resource utilization, ultimately enhancing the sustainability and stewardship of healthcare systems.

5.5 HEALTHCARE STEWARDSHIP'S IMPACT ON LIFECOURSE HEALTH DEVELOPMENT

Foundational Elements of Life-Course Health Development. Life course health development (LCHD) is a framework that emphasizes the importance of understanding health across the entire span of a person's life, from prenatal development through old age (Simmons et al., 2024). At its core, LCHD recognizes that health is influenced by a complex interplay of biological, behavioral, psychological, and social factors that accumulate over time (Halfon et al., 2002; Halfon et al., 2014; Halfon et al., 2018a; Halfon et al., 2018b).

One foundational element of LCHD is the concept of developmental plasticity, which suggests that early life experiences, including prenatal conditions and childhood environments, can have long-lasting effects on health outcomes later in life. This principle underscores the importance of early interventions and proactive measures to produce positive health and optimize wellness and well-being across the life span.

Another key element of LCHD is the recognition of critical or sensitive periods during development when individuals may be particularly susceptible to the effects of environmental exposures or interventions. For example, fetal development and early childhood are recognized as critical periods during which factors like nutrition, exposure to toxins, and social interactions can profoundly influence life course health trajectories. Understanding these critical periods allows healthcare providers and policymakers to prioritize interventions that can have the greatest impact on improving health outcomes and reducing health disparities across different populations.

Additionally, LCHD emphasizes the dynamic nature of health development throughout the life course. Health is viewed as a continuous process of adaptation and resilience in response to changing circumstances and environments. This perspective encourages healthcare providers to adopt a proactive approach to medical care that considers individuals' evolving needs, preferences, and values and capacities at different stages of life. By promoting healthy lifestyle and behaviors, providing early interventions, and addressing social determinants of health across the life course, healthcare delivery systems can support individuals in achieving and maintaining optimal health outcomes throughout their lives. Striving to enhance both the quality and quantity of their health span to match or even exceed their lifespan is a dynamic process for individuals during the aging process.

Moreover, LCHD emphasizes the importance of a life course perspective in healthy public policy development and healthcare delivery. Healthy public policies that support early childhood education, maternal and child health, healthy aging, and social welfare programs can have significant impacts on population health, wellness, and well-being across generations. Integrating LCHD principles into public health strategies and healthcare systems can help address health inequities, promote health equity, and improve overall population health outcomes. Embracing a life course approach to health development ensures that healthcare systems and healthy public policies are responsive to the diverse and evolving needs of individuals and communities across their lifespans.

Implementing LCHD poses several significant challenges for healthcare delivery systems and policymakers aiming to adopt this holistic, integrated, and comprehensive approach to health across the lifespan. One of the primary hurdles is the complexity of addressing health determinants that accumulate over time. LCHD emphasizes the impact of early life experiences, social determinants of health, and environmental factors on lifelong health outcomes. However, addressing these factors requires a multi-sectoral strategy and approach involving collaboration among healthcare providers, educators, social services, policymakers, and community organizations. Coordinating efforts across different sectors and disciplines can be challenging due to differing priorities, funding streams, and administrative structures, which can hinder the seamless integration of services and resources needed to support LCHD initiatives effectively.

Another critical challenge is the need for longitudinal data and empirically-supported evidence-based research to inform LCHD policies and interventions. Understanding the long-term effects of early life exposures and interventions requires robust data collection methods and longitudinal studies that track health outcomes over time. However, gathering and analyzing such data can be resource-intensive and time-consuming. Furthermore, translating research findings into actionable healthy public policies and practices that promote health equity and improve population health outcomes requires bridging the gap between education, research, policy, and practice, which can be challenging in open, adaptive, and complex healthcare delivery systems.

Additionally, promoting intergenerational health and addressing health disparities across diverse populations are central goals of LCHD. However, achieving health equity requires addressing systemic inequalities in access to healthcare, education, housing, and economic opportunities. These social determinants of health significantly impact health outcomes and contribute to disparities in health outcomes across different population groups. Implementing LCHD initiatives that effectively reduce health disparities requires targeted interventions, culturally competent care, and healthy public policies that address the root causes of social inequities.

Furthermore, sustaining political and public support for LCHD initiatives presents ongoing challenges. LCHD requires long-term investments in proactive care, early interventions, and social support programs that may not yield immediate results but are critical for promoting lifelong health, wellness, and well-being. Securing funding, garnering political will, and maintaining public engagement in LCHD efforts can be challenging amidst competing priorities and budget constraints. Building consensus among stakeholders, advocating for evidence-based healthy public policies, and demonstrating the long-term benefits of LCHD approaches are essential strategies for overcoming these challenges and fostering sustainable improvements in population health outcomes.

Life-course Health Development significantly impacts healthcare stewardship by recognizing that health outcomes are shaped by a complex interplay of biological, behavioral, social, and environmental factors throughout an individual's life. This perspective encourages early interventions and sustained support across various life stages, aiming to produce positive health trajectories from preconception to old age. By focusing on critical periods of development and the cumulative effects of experiences and exposures, LCHD promotes proactive care strategies. This long-term approach helps prevent the onset of chronic diseases, reduces the need for intensive and costly medical interventions, and ensures more efficient allocation of healthcare resources, thus enhancing healthcare stewardship.

Furthermore, LCHD emphasizes the importance of addressing health disparities and promoting equity by considering the social determinants of health. This approach advocates for healthy public policies and programs that support healthy environments, access to quality education, economic stability, and social cohesion, which are essential for fostering long-term health, wellness, and well-being. By investing in early childhood development, maternal health, and community health initiatives, LCHD aims to create a foundation for healthier populations. This investment in upstream determinants of health leads to a more sustainable healthcare system, as it reduces the burden of chronic conditions and associated healthcare costs in the long term. By prioritizing health, wellness, and well-being across the lifespan, LCHD supports a more strategic and effective use of healthcare resources, ensuring better stewardship and improved health outcomes for all.

5.6 HEALTHCARE STEWARDSHIP'S IMPACT ON THE EXISTENTIAL THREATS TO THE AMERICAN HEALTHCARE DELIVERY SYSTEM

Existential threats to the American healthcare system profoundly impact healthcare stewardship, which is the responsible management and allocation of resources to ensure optimal patient care discussed earlier in Chapter 1. One significant impact is the strain on financial stewardship. Rising healthcare costs compel administrators to make difficult decisions about where to allocate limited funds. This often leads to prioritizing immediate needs over long-term investments and infrastructure improvements. As a result, the system becomes reactive rather than proactive, with resources disproportionately directed toward acute and emergency care instead of addressing underlying causes of poor health, wellness, and well-being which undermines the sustainability of healthcare delivery.

The increasing burden of chronic diseases exacerbates the challenge of stewardship by demanding substantial resources for ongoing management and treatment. Chronic conditions require continuous monitoring, medications, and interventions, consuming a significant portion of healthcare budgets. This continuous demand diverts resources from other areas, such as education, practice, innovation, research, and the development of new treatments and technology. Moreover, it highlights the need for effective public health strategies and essential public health services, which are often underfunded and under-utilized. Inadequate investment in the essential public health services not only perpetuates the cycle of chronic illness but also places a continuous strain on healthcare delivery systems, limiting their ability to respond to new and emerging health threats.

The post-COVID-19 healthcare workforce crisis further complicates stewardship efforts. The shortage of healthcare professionals' forces healthcare organizations to realign workforce management strategies, often leading to increased workloads for existing staff, potential compromises in patient care quality, and higher operational costs due to the need for temporary staffing solutions. Ensuring effective stewardship in this context requires innovative approaches to workforce development, such as investing in health system science education and training programs, improving job satisfaction and retention, and exploring new models of care delivery that maximize the efficiency and impact of available healthcare professionals.

Technological advancements and cybersecurity threats present a dual-edged challenge to healthcare stewardship. On one hand, advanced medical technology has the potential to significantly enhance care delivery through improved data management, telemedicine, and personalized treatments. On the other hand, these advancements introduce new risks and resource allocation dilemmas. Investing in cybersecurity measures to protect patient privacy and system integrity is crucial but often expensive. Balancing the cost of safeguarding against cyber threats with the benefits of technological innovation requires careful and strategic stewardship to ensure that resources are used effectively and that patient care remains uncompromised.

Lastly, political and regulatory instability adds a layer of complexity to healthcare stewardship. Frequent changes in public policies and regulations create uncertainty, making it difficult for healthcare organizations to plan long-term strategies and investments. The constant flux in funding and regulatory requirements forces healthcare leaders to be adaptable and resourceful, often prioritizing short-term compliance over strategic leadership, governance, and development. Effective stewardship in this environment demands a clear mission and vision and strong leadership to navigate the political landscape, advocate for stable and supportive healthy public policies, and ensure that resources are directed towards sustainable improvements in healthcare delivery.

5.7 US HOSPITALS AND HEALTHCARE SYSTEMS BENEFIT FROM HEALTHCARE STEWARDSHIP

Healthcare stewardship involves the responsible planning and management of healthcare resources to ensure sustainability, efficiency, and improved patient outcomes. Hospitals and healthcare systems can greatly benefit from implementing robust healthcare stewardship programs (He et al., 2022, Chan et al., 2019; Di Pentima et al., 2011; Logan et al., 2019; Buckel et al., 2018). By focusing on optimizing resource allocation, these institutions can reduce waste and lower costs while maintaining high standards of patient care. This can involve adopting empirically-supported evidence-based practices for treatments and interventions, ensuring that medications and technologies are used appropriately and effectively. Additionally, stewardship programs can help streamline operations, leading to more efficient use of staff time and hospital facilities, ultimately enhancing the overall patient experience.

Another key benefit of healthcare stewardship is the promotion of patient safety and the reduction of medical errors. By establishing clear protocols and guidelines for the use of antibiotics, for instance, hospitals can combat the rise of antibiotic-resistant infections, which are a significant public health concern. Stewardship efforts also emphasize the importance of continuous education and training for healthcare professionals, ensuring they are up-to-date with the latest best practices and innovations in patient care. This ongoing professional development can lead to improved clinical outcomes and a more knowledgeable and skilled workforce, capable of delivering high-quality care.

Moreover, healthcare stewardship can improve patient trust in the healthcare system. When patients receive appropriate, timely, truthful, and effective care, their overall experience is enhanced, which can lead to better patient compliance and health outcomes. Stewardship initiatives often involve patient education programs that empower individuals to take an active role in their own health management. By fostering a collaborative approach between healthcare providers and patients, hospitals can build stronger relationships and community trust.

Lastly, effective healthcare stewardship can enhance the reputation and financial stability of hospitals and healthcare systems. As these institutions become known for their commitment to quality care and efficient resource use, they are likely to attract more patients and potential partnerships. Financially, the reduction in unnecessary procedures, hospital readmissions, and extended hospital stays can lead to significant cost savings. These savings can be reinvested into further improving patient care, updating facilities, and expanding services, creating a positive cycle of continuous improvement and sustainability.

5.8 HEALTHCARE STEWARDSHIP AND VALUE-BASED HEALTHCARE IN THE US

Value-based healthcare and healthcare stewardship are closely aligned concepts that emphasize efficiency, quality, and patient outcomes (Moleman et al., 2022; Williams et al., 2024). Value-based healthcare focuses on delivering care that improves health outcomes relative to the cost of providing that care (Porter, 2010). This model shifts the emphasis from volume to value, incentivizing healthcare providers to prioritize treatments and interventions that deliver the best outcomes for patients. By emphasizing quality over quantity of medical care, value-based healthcare aligns naturally with the principles of healthcare stewardship, which advocate for the responsible management and allocation of healthcare resources to maximize patient benefits and system efficiency.

One of the key ways value-based healthcare enhances healthcare stewardship is through the implementation of outcome-based reimbursement models (Kaplan et al., 2011). In these models, providers are rewarded for achieving specific health outcomes rather than for the number of services rendered. This encourages providers to adopt best practices, evidence-based treatments, and coordinated care pathways that improve patient health while avoiding unnecessary tests and procedures. As a result, healthcare resources are used more judiciously, reducing waste and lowering costs. This approach not only enhances the financial sustainability of healthcare systems but also ensures that patients receive care that is both effective and necessary.

Value-based healthcare also promotes the integration of medical care across different providers and settings, a critical aspect of healthcare stewardship. Coordinated care models, such as accountable care organizations (ACOs) and patient-centered medical homes (PCMHs), focus on delivering seamless, comprehensive care to patients, particularly those with chronic conditions or complex health needs. By fostering collaboration among primary care providers, specialists, and other healthcare professionals, these models of care reduce fragmentation and duplication of healthcare services. This integrated approach leads to better health outcomes and more efficient use of resources, as care is managed holistically rather than in isolated silos.

Patient engagement and empowerment are central to both value-based healthcare and healthcare stewardship. In a value-based model, patients are encouraged to take an active role in their own health management, supported by education, resources, and shared decision-making with their healthcare providers. This empowerment leads to better adherence to treatment plans, healthier lifestyles, and more informed choices about care options. Engaged patients are more likely to participate in proactive care and early intervention, which can prevent the progression of diseases and reduce the need for costly acute care services. By fostering patient engagement, value-based healthcare contributes to the efficient and effective use of healthcare resources, a cornerstone of healthcare stewardship.

Moreover, value-based healthcare supports the use of data and analytics to drive continuous quality improvement in healthcare delivery. Advanced data analytics enable providers to track and measure outcomes, identify gaps in care, and implement targeted interventions. This data-driven approach ensures that healthcare resources are directed toward areas where they can have the greatest impact, enhancing the overall effectiveness of medical care. By leveraging data, healthcare organizations can also monitor the performance of different interventions and adapt strategies in real-time to improve patient outcomes and resource utilization. This continuous cycle of measurement and improvement is a key aspect of both value-based healthcare and healthcare stewardship.

In summary, value-based healthcare and healthcare stewardship share a common goal of optimizing healthcare delivery to achieve the best possible outcomes for patients while ensuring the sustainable use of resources. By prioritizing high-quality care at the lowest cost through the integration of medical care, patient engagement, and data utilization, value-based healthcare models support the principles of stewardship and contribute to a more efficient, effective, and equitable healthcare system. As healthcare delivery systems continue to evolve, the alignment of these two approaches will be essential for addressing the complex challenges of modern healthcare and improving the overall health, wellness, and well-being of populations.

5.9 REFERENCES

Buckel, W. R., Veillette, J. J., Vento, T. J., et al. (2018) Antimicrobial stewardship in community hospitals. *Medical Clinics* 102 (5), 913-928.

Chan, B. T., Veillard, J. H., Cowling, K., et al. (2019) Stewardship of quality of care in health systems: Core functions, common pitfalls, and potential solutions. *Public Administration and Development* 39 (1): 34-46.

Chim, C., Connor, S., Law, P. M. More than just diet and exercise: social determinants of health and well-being. *Public Health in Pharmacy Practice*, 69.

Di Pentima, M. C., Chan, S., Hossain, J. (2011) Benefits of a pediatric antimicrobial stewardship program at a children's hospital. *Pediatrics* 128 (6): 1062-1070.

Halfon, N., Hochstein, M. (2002) Life course health development: an integrated framework for developing health, policy, and research. *The Milbank Quarterly* 80 (3): 433-479.

Halfon, N., Larson, K., Lu, M., et al. (2014) Lifecourse health development: past, present and future. *Maternal and Child Health Journal* 18: 344-365.

Halfon, N., Forrest, C. B., Lerner, R. M., et al. (2018a) *Handbook of life course health development.* Springer.

Halfon, N., Forrest, C. B. (2018b) The emerging theoretical framework of life course health development.*Handbook of Life Course Health Development* 19-43.

He, A. J., Bali, A. S., Ramesh, M. (2022) Active stewardship in healthcare: Lessons from China's health policy reforms.*Social Policy& Administration*56 (6): 925-940.

Kaplan, R. S., Porter, M. E. (2011) How to solve the cost crisis in health care.*Harv Bus Rev* 89 (9): 46-52.

Krieger, N. (2024).*Epidemiology and the people's health: theory and context.* Oxford University Press.

Logan, A. Y., Williamson, J. E., Reinke, et al. (2019) Establishing an antimicrobial stewardship collaborative across a large, diverse health care system.*The Joint Commission Journal on Quality and Patient Safety* 45 (9): 591-599.

Moleman, M., Zuiderent-Jerak, T., Lageweg, M., et al. (2022) Doctors as resource stewards? Translating high-value, cost-conscious care to the consulting room.*Health Care Analysis*30 (3): 215-239.

Omri, N. O., Al Masry, Z., Giampiccolo, et al. (2019) Data management requirements for PHM implementation in SMEs. *Prognostics and System Health Management Conference (PHM-Paris)*232-238.

Porter, M. E. (2010). What is value in health care?*New England Journal of Medicine* 363 (26): 2477-2481.

Santana, M. J., Manalili, K., Jolley, R. Jet al. (2018) How to practice person-centred care: A conceptual framework.*Health Expectations*21 (2), 429-440.

Skochelak, A.E., Hammoud, M.M., Lomis, K.D. (2021) Health Systems Science, 2nd Edition. Philadelphia, PA: Elsevier.

Simmons, D., Gupta, Y., Hernandez, T. L., et al. (2024). Call to action for a life course approach.*The Lancet.* Access@ https://doi.org/10.1016/S0140-6736 (24)00826-2.

van Vooren, N.J., Steenkamer, B.M., Baan, H.W. et al. (2020) Transforming towards sustainable health and wellbeing systems: Eight guiding principles based on the experiences of nine Dutch Population Health Management initiatives. *Health Policy* 124 (1): 37-43.

Williams, S. B., McCaffrey, P., Reynoso, et al. (2024) Implementation of a High-Value, Evidence-Based Care Program: Impact and Opportunities for Learning Organizations.*Journal of Healthcare Management*69 (4): 296-308.

World Health Organization. (2015a).WHO global strategy on people-centred and integrated health services: interim report(No. WHO/HIS/SDS/2015.6).

World Health Organization. (2015b). People-centred and integrated health services: an overview of the evidence: interim report.

World Health Organization. (2018). Continuity and coordination of care: a practice brief to support implementation of the WHO Framework on integrated people-centred health services.

CHAPTER 6

US PUBLIC HEALTH SYSTEM ESSENTIAL SERVICES AND FUNCTIONS

6.1 THE ESSENTIAL SERVICES AND FUNCTIONS OF THE US PUBLIC HEALTH SYSTEM

The U.S. Public Health System is essential in maintaining and improving the health, wellness, and well-being of the public-at-large through a comprehensive array of services and functions (Rosen, 2015; DeSalvo et al., 2021; Goldsteen et al., 2024).

At its core, the public health system is dedicated to preventing disease, prolonging life, and promoting health, wellness, and well-being through organized community efforts. One of the fundamental services it provides is disease prevention and control, which involves monitoring and addressing infectious disease outbreaks, managing chronic diseases, and implementing vaccination programs. This surveillance and rapid response capability are crucial in mitigating the spread of diseases and protecting the public's health.

Another critical function of the U.S. Public Health System is health education and promotion. This involves disseminating information and resources to educate the public about health risks, healthy behaviors, and proactive measures. Public health campaigns on topics such as smoking cessation, healthy eating, and exercise play a vital role in reducing the incidence of lifestyle-related diseases and improving overall community health. Additionally, public health agencies work to promote health equity by addressing social determinants of health and ensuring that vulnerable populations have access to the resources and services they need to lead healthier lives.

Environmental health is another key service provided by the public health system. This includes monitoring and regulating environmental factors that can impact health, such as air and water quality, food safety, and hazardous waste. Public health professionals conduct inspections, enforce regulations, and respond to environmental hazards to protect communities from harmful exposures. By ensuring a safe and healthy environment, the public health system helps prevent a wide range of diseases and conditions.

The public health system also plays a vital role in disaster preparedness and response. Public health agencies collaborate with other government agencies and community-based organizations to develop and implement emergency plans for natural disasters, pandemics, and bioterrorism events. This includes ensuring that there are adequate resources, such as medical supplies and personnel, and that there is a coordinated response to protect the health and safety of the public-at-large. Effective preparedness and response strategies are essential in minimizing the impact of emergencies on public health.

Overall, the U.S. Public Health System performs a wide array of essential services and functions that are critical to protecting and promoting the health of the US public. Through disease prevention and control, health education and promotion, environmental health, and disaster preparedness and response, the public health system works to create healthy and well communities and improve the quality of life and well-being for all Americans.

6.2 INNOVATIONS IN THE AMERICAN PUBLIC HEALTH SYSTEM DOMAIN

Public health innovations have significantly transformed the landscape of health and wellness, improved outcomes and enhancing the quality of life on a global scale (Rilkoff et al., 2024). These innovations span various domains, from advanced technology and data analytics to healthy public policy and community-based interventions, each contributing to the advancement of public health.

One of the most significant public health innovations is the development and widespread implementation of vaccines (Cable et al., 2020). Vaccination programs have been instrumental in controlling and eradicating infectious diseases such as smallpox, polio, and measles. The rapid development and distribution of COVID-19 vaccines is a recent example, demonstrating the power of scientific advancements and global collaboration in addressing public health crises. These efforts not only save millions of lives but also prevent the spread of diseases, contributing to the overall health of populations.

Telehealth and digital health technologies represent another major innovation in public health (Gunasekeran et al., 2021). Telehealth allows for remote consultations and monitoring, expanding access to healthcare services, especially in underserved and rural areas. Mobile health applications and wearable devices enable individuals to track their health metrics, manage chronic conditions, and receive timely health information. These technologies empower patients to take control of their health and facilitate more efficient and effective healthcare delivery.

Data analytics and big data have revolutionized public health by enhancing the ability to predict, monitor, and respond to health issues. Advanced data analytics tools allow public health professionals to identify patterns and trends in health data, enabling proactive measures and targeted interventions. For instance, predictive analytics can forecast disease outbreaks, helping authorities to implement preventive measures swiftly. Additionally, big data can inform policy decisions and resource allocation, ensuring that public health initiatives are evidence-based and impactful (Sarker et al., 2021).

Community-based interventions and participatory approaches are also key innovations in public health (Nickel et al., 2020; Faber et al., 2021). Programs that engage communities in the planning and implementation of health initiatives are more likely to be successful and sustainable. Examples include community health worker programs, which leverage local knowledge and trust to deliver health education and services, and participatory research projects that involve community members in identifying health priorities and developing solutions (Kane et al., 2021). These approaches foster a sense of ownership and empowerment, leading to more effective and culturally appropriate public health interventions.

Finally, advancements in genomics and personalized medicine are paving the way for more tailored public health strategies (Yurkovich et al., 2024). Understanding the genetic factors that influence health and disease can lead to more precise prevention and treatment plans. For example, genetic screening programs can identify individuals at high risk for certain diseases, allowing for early intervention and personalized care plans that improve health outcomes and reduce healthcare costs.

In summary, public health innovations in vaccines, digital health, data analytics, community-based interventions, and genomics are driving significant improvements in health outcomes. These advancements enable more efficient, effective, and equitable public health strategies, ultimately contributing to the health, wellness, and well-being of Americans and the global population-at-large.

6.3 THE IMPORTANCE OF A STRONG US PUBLIC HEALTH SYSTEM FOCUSED ON HEALTHCARE STEWARDSHIP

Public health departments play a critical role in healthcare stewardship by serving as a central hub for coordinating efforts across various healthcare providers and community organizations (Aragon et al., 2015). They help develop and implement public health policies and programs that ensure the efficient use of resources and promote the health, wellness, and well-being of the population. By conducting comprehensive health needs assessments and collecting data on health outcomes, public health departments can identify areas where resources are most needed and develop targeted interventions to address those needs. This strategic planning helps to allocate resources more effectively, preventing waste and ensuring that efforts are directed toward the most impactful areas.

In addition, public health departments are instrumental in promoting proactive care and health education, which are key components of healthcare stewardship. They lead campaigns and initiatives to raise awareness about the importance of vaccination, regular health screenings, healthy lifestyles, and disease prevention. By educating the public and encouraging proactive health management, public health departments help to reduce the incidence of chronic conditions that can place a significant burden on healthcare delivery systems. This proactive approach not only improves individual health outcomes but also decreases the overall demand for healthcare services, thus optimizing the use of available resources (Caron et al., 2023).

Public health departments also play a vital role in managing and responding to public health emergencies, such as infectious disease outbreaks and natural disasters. Their ability to quickly mobilize resources, disseminate information, and coordinate with various stakeholders is crucial in mitigating the impact of such events. Effective emergency preparedness and response plans developed by public health departments ensure that healthcare resources are used efficiently and that the community receives timely and appropriate care. This level of preparedness is a fundamental aspect of healthcare stewardship, as it helps to prevent the overwhelming of healthcare systems during crises (Rose et al., 2017).

Furthermore, public health departments foster collaboration and partnerships among different sectors, including healthcare providers, government agencies, non-profit organizations, and the private sector. By bringing together diverse stakeholders, they create a more integrated and cohesive healthcare delivery system that can share resources, knowledge, and best practices. This collaborative approach enhances the overall effectiveness and efficiency of healthcare delivery, ensuring that resources are used wisely and that patients receive high-quality care. Public health departments act as a catalyst for innovation and improvement, continually seeking ways to enhance healthcare stewardship through education, practice, research, policy development, and community engagement.

6.4 THE ESSENTIALS OF COMMUNITY-BASED ORGANIZATIONS

Community-based organizations (CBOs) play an essential role in addressing local needs and enhancing the quality of life within communities (Wilson et al., 2012). These organizations are typically nonprofit entities that operate at the grassroots level, providing a wide range of services and support tailored to the specific needs of their communities. By leveraging local knowledge and resources, CBOs are uniquely positioned to respond effectively to various social, economic, and health challenges.

One of the primary functions of CBOs is to offer direct services and support to community members (Taylor et al., 2021). This can include providing food assistance, housing support, job training, healthcare services, and educational programs. For instance, food banks and meal programs run by CBOs ensure that individuals and families facing food insecurity have access to nutritious meals. Similarly, CBOs offering housing assistance help prevent homelessness by providing shelter, rental assistance, and supportive housing services. These direct services are crucial in meeting the immediate needs of vulnerable populations and promoting overall community well-being.

Another critical function of CBOs is advocacy and community organizing (Truong et al., 2023). CBOs often serve as advocates for their communities, working to influence public policy and bring about systemic changes that address the root causes of social and economic inequalities. By mobilizing community members and building coalitions,

CBOs can amplify the voices of marginalized groups and push for policy reforms that promote social justice and equity. For example, CBOs may advocate for affordable housing policies, improved access to healthcare, or educational reforms that benefit underserved communities.

CBOs also play a vital role in fostering social cohesion and community engagement (Habermann et al., 2014). They provide spaces for community members to come together, share experiences, and collaborate on initiatives that improve their neighborhoods. Through community meetings, cultural events, and volunteer opportunities, CBOs help build a sense of belonging and collective responsibility among residents. This social capital is essential for creating resilient communities that can effectively address challenges and leverage opportunities for growth and development.

Furthermore, CBOs often serve as intermediaries between communities and larger institutions, such as government agencies, healthcare providers, and philanthropic organizations (Franks et al., 2017). By acting as a bridge, CBOs ensure that community needs and perspectives are considered in decision-making processes. They also help facilitate access to resources and services provided by these institutions, ensuring that they reach the individuals who need them the most. For instance, CBOs might partner with healthcare providers to offer community health screenings or work with local governments to implement neighborhood improvement projects.

In summary, community-based organizations are indispensable in addressing the diverse needs of their communities through direct services, advocacy, community engagement, and acting as intermediaries with larger institutions. Their grassroots approach and deep understanding of local contexts enable them to effectively respond to challenges, promote social cohesion, and drive positive change at the community level.

6.5 ENGAGING COMMUNITY-BASED ORGANIZATIONS IN HEALTHCARE STEWARDSHIP

Engaging community-based organizations (CBOs) in healthcare stewardship is a powerful strategy to enhance the effectiveness and reach of healthcare initiatives. CBOs have deep roots within their communities and possess a thorough understanding of local needs, cultures, and challenges. By collaborating with these organizations, healthcare providers can leverage this local knowledge to design and implement more effective health programs and interventions. CBOs can serve as trusted intermediaries, helping to bridge the gap between healthcare systems and the populations they serve, ensuring that healthcare services are accessible, acceptable, and appropriate for diverse community members (Franks et al., 2017).

One of the key benefits of involving CBOs in healthcare stewardship is the ability to improve health literacy and empower individuals to take an active role in managing their health (Palumbo et al., 2018; Sorenson et al., 2021). CBOs often have established communication channels, trustworthiness, and truthfulness within the community, making them ideal partners for disseminating information about proactive health, healthy lifestyles and behaviors, and available healthcare services. This grassroots approach can lead to better health outcomes and reduced healthcare costs by preventing illnesses and managing chronic conditions more effectively.

CBOs also play a critical role in addressing social determinants of health, which are key factors in healthcare stewardship (Taylor et al., 2021). Issues such as housing, education, employment, and food security significantly impact health outcomes. CBOs are often involved in these areas and can provide comprehensive support that addresses both health and social needs. By partnering with CBOs, healthcare providers can adopt a holistic, integrated, and comprehensive approach to people-centered care, mixing social services with medical care to address the root causes of health issues. This collaborative approach can lead to more sustainable health improvements and a more efficient use of healthcare resources.

Furthermore, engaging CBOs can enhance the cultural competence of healthcare delivery (Garrido et al., 2019). CBOs often have staff and volunteers who are part of the communities they serve, bringing valuable cultural insights and language skills to healthcare interactions. This cultural competence is crucial for building trust, improving patient-provider communication, and ensuring that healthcare services are culturally appropriate. By incorporating the perspectives and expertise of CBOs, healthcare providers can develop and deliver services that are more responsive to the cultural needs of diverse populations, leading to better patient satisfaction and adherence to treatment plans.

Involving CBOs in healthcare stewardship also facilitates community-driven health initiatives, empowering communities to take ownership of their health outcomes (Schensul et al., 2014). CBOs can help organize and support community health boards, advisory councils, and participatory research projects, giving community members a voice in the planning, implementation, and evaluation of health programs. This participatory approach ensures that health initiatives are aligned with community priorities and are more likely to be sustainable in the long term. It also fosters a sense of ownership and accountability among community members, encouraging active participation in proactive health services efforts.

Lastly, partnerships with CBOs can strengthen the overall resilience of healthcare systems (Koch et al., 2017). During public health emergencies, such as natural disasters or infectious disease outbreaks, CBOs can provide essential support by mobilizing community resources, disseminating information, and coordinating local response efforts. Their established presence and trust within the community enable them to act swiftly and effectively, complementing the efforts of the medical community and local public health districts. By integrating CBOs into emergency preparedness and response plans, healthcare delivery systems, public health agencies, and emergency management systems can enhance their capacity to respond to crises and ensure continuity of care for marginalized individuals and vulnerable populations.

In summary, engaging community-based organizations in healthcare stewardship brings numerous benefits including improved health literacy, holistic, integrated, and comprehensive medical care addressing social determinants of health, enhanced cultural competence, community-driven health initiatives, and strengthened multi-system resilience. These partnerships create a more inclusive, effective, and sustainable healthcare system that is better equipped to meet the needs of diverse communities and address the complex challenges of modern healthcare.

6.6 PUBLIC HEALTH AND COMMUNITY-BASED ORGANIZATIONS: SYNERGIES IN HEALTHCARE STEWARDSHIP

The relationship between public health entities and community-based organizations (CBOs) is dynamic and critical for addressing the health needs of populations effectively (Acosta et al., 2018). Public health agencies, such as departments of health at local, state, and national levels, play a pivotal role in promoting and protecting the health of communities through policy development, surveillance, health education, and proactive disease initiatives. On the other hand, CBOs operate at the grassroots level and are deeply embedded within communities, often specializing in delivering targeted health services, advocacy, and social support to specific populations or addressing particular health issues.

One of the key dynamics in this relationship is collaboration and partnership. Public health agencies often collaborate with CBOs to leverage their expertise, community trust, and cultural competence in implementing health interventions (Agonafer et al., 2021). CBOs, in turn, benefit from public health resources, technical support, and access to data and evidence-based practices that enhance their effectiveness. Effective collaboration fosters a shared understanding of community needs, strengthens the capacity to address health disparities, and maximizes the impact of interventions by combining resources and expertise.

Another dynamic is the role of CBOs in advocating for community health needs and influencing public health policies (Allen et al., 2021). CBOs are uniquely positioned to advocate for policies that address social determinants of health, promote health equity, and address the specific needs of marginalized or underserved populations (Winton et al., 2018). They serve as a bridge between communities and public health authorities, advocating for community priorities and ensuring that public health initiatives are culturally responsive and inclusive. This advocacy role is crucial in shaping policies that support community well-being and foster sustainable improvements in population health outcomes.

Challenges also exist in this relationship, including resource constraints, communication barriers, and differing organizational priorities. Public health agencies may face limitations in funding and capacity, impacting their ability to support and sustain partnerships with CBOs effectively. Communication challenges, such as differing terminology or bureaucratic processes, can hinder effective collaboration and coordination of efforts. Moreover, aligning organizational priorities and goals between public health agencies and diverse CBOs with varying missions and objectives requires ongoing dialogue, mutual respect, and commitment to shared goals (Yasmin et al., 2022).

Overall, navigating the relationship between public health and CBOs involves recognizing and leveraging each other's strengths, fostering trust, truthfulness, and collaboration, and addressing challenges through effective communication and strategic partnerships. By working together synergistically, public health agencies and CBOs can enhance their collective impact to produce positive health, optimize wellness, and improve the well-being of communities, particularly those facing health disparities and social inequities.

6.7 REFERENCES

Acosta, J. D., Burgette, L., Chandra, et al. (2018) How community and public health partnerships contribute to disaster recovery and resilience.*Disaster Medicine and Public Health Preparedness*12 (5): 635-643.

Agonafer, E. P., Carson, S. L., Nunez, V., et al. (2021) Community-based organizations' perspectives on improving health and social service integration.*BMC Public Health*21: 1-12.

Allen, E. H., Haley, J. M., Aarons, J., et al. (2021) *Leveraging community expertise to advance health equity.*Washington, DC: Urban Institute.

Aragón, T. J., Garcia, B. A., et al. (2015) Designing a learning health organization for collective impact. *JPHMP* 21 (Suppl 1): S24–S33.

Cable, J., Srikantiah, P., Crowe Jr, et al. (2020) Vaccine innovations for emerging infectious diseases—a symposium report.*Annals of the New York Academy of Sciences* 1462 (1): 14-26.

Caron, R. M., Noel, K., Reed, R. N., et al. (2023) Health Promotion, Health Protection, and Disease Prevention: Challenges and Opportunities in a Dynamic Landscape.*AJPM*3 (1): 100167.

DeSalvo, K. B., Kadakia, K. T. (2021). Public Health 3.0 after COVID-19—reboot or upgrade?*American Journal of Public Health*111 (S3): S179-S181.

Faber, J. S., Al-Dhahir, I., Reijnders, T., et al. (2021). Attitudes toward health, healthcare, and eHealth of people with a low socioeconomic status: a community-based participatory approach.*Frontiers in Digital Health* 3: 690182.

Franks, R. P., Bory, C. T. (2017) Strategies for developing intermediary organizations: Considerations for practice.*Families in Society* 98 (1): 27-34.

Garrido, R., Garcia-Ramirez, M., Balcazar, F. E. (2019) Moving towards community cultural competence. *International Journal of Intercultural Relations* 73: 89-101.

Goldsteen, R. L., Goldsteen, K., Dwelle, T. (2024). Introduction to public health: promises and practices. 2nd Edition. New York, NY: Springer Publishing.

Gunasekeran, D. V., Tseng, R. M. W. W., Tham, et al. (2021) Applications of digital health for public health responses to COVID-19: a systematic scoping review of artificial intelligence, telehealth and related technologies. *NPJ Digital Medicine* 4 (1): 40.

Habermann, H., Mackie, C. D., Prewitt, K. (Eds.). (2014) *Civic engagement and social cohesion: Measuring dimensions of social capital to inform policy* Washington, DC: National Academies Press.

Kane, S., Radkar, A., Gadgil, M., et al. (2021) Community health workers as influential health system actors and not" just another pair of hands". *International Journal of Health Policy and Management* 10 (8): 465.

Koch, H., Franco, Z. E., O'Sullivan, T., et al. (2017) Community views of the federal emergency management agency's "whole community" strategy in a complex US City: Re-envisioning societal resilience. *Technological Forecasting and Social Change* 121: 31-38.

Nickel, S., von dem Knesebeck, O. (2020) Effectiveness of community-based health promotion interventions in urban areas: a systematic review. *Journal of Community Health* 45 (2): 419-434.

Palumbo, R., Annarumma, C. (2018) Empowering organizations to empower patients: An organizational health literacy approach. *International Journal of Healthcare Management* 11 (2): 133-142.

Rilkoff, H., Struck, S., Ziegler, C., et al. (2024) Innovations in public health surveillance: An overview of novel use of data and analytic methods.*Canada Communicable Disease Report* 50 (3-4): 93–101.

Rose, D. A., Murthy, S., Brooks, J., et al. (2017) The Evolution of Public Health Emergency Management as a Field of Practice. *American Journal of Public Health*107 (S2): S126–S133. https://doi.org/10.2105/AJPH.2017.303947

Rosen, G. (2015).*A history of public health.* Jhu Press.

Sarker, I. H. (2021) Data science and analytics: an overview from data-driven smart computing, decision-making and applications perspective.*SN Computer Science*2 (5): 377.

Schensul, S. L., Schensul, J. J., Singer, M., et al. (2014) Participatory methods and community-based collaborations.*Handbook of Methods in Cultural Anthropology*2:185-212.

Sorensen, K., Levin-Zamir, D., Duong, T. V., et al. (2021) Building health literacy system capacity: a framework for health literate systems.*Health Promotion International*36 (Suppl): i13-i23.

Taylor, L. A., Byhoff, E. (2021) Money moves the mare: the response of community-based organizations to health care's embrace of social determinants.*The Milbank Quarterly*99 (1): 171-208.

Truong, J., Sandhu, P., Sheng, et al. (2023) Advocacy in community-based service learning: perspectives of community partner organizations.*Canadian Medical Education Journal*14 (1): 90-94.

Wilson, M. G., Lavis, J. N., Guta, A. (2012) Community-based organizations in the health sector: a scoping review.*Health Research Policy and Systems*10: 1-9.

Winton, S., Evans, M. P. (2018) Consulting, mediating, conducting, and supporting: How community-based organizations engage with research to influence policy. Pp 4-25. *In*Engaging Families, Educators, and Communities as Educational Advocates:Routledge.

Yasmin, S., Haque, R., Kadambaya, K., et al. (2022) Exploring how public health partnerships with community-based organizations (CBOs) can be leveraged for health promotion and community health.*INQUIRY: The Journal of Health Care Organization, Provision, and Financing* 59: 00469580221139372.

Yurkovich, J. T., Evans, S. J., Rappaport, N., et al. (2024) The transition from genomics to phenomics in personalized population health. *Nature Reviews Genetics* 25 (4): 286-302.

CHAPTER 7

THE MEDICAL COMMONS

7.1 THE TRAGEDY OF THE COMMONS

Garrett Hardin (1968) in a landmark article, *The Tragedy of the Commons*, published in *Science*, described a class of human problems that had no technical solutions. He stated, "A technical solution may be defined as one that requires a change only in the techniques of the natural sciences, demanding little or nothing in the way of change in human values or ideas of morality." Hardin was discussing the issues related to population growth. He summarized that even with an infinite amount of energy available to sustain an ever-expanding population, individual and community interests compete for these energy resources. This results in behavioral issues, both positive and negative, that cannot sustain the population forever. Hardin developed a hypothetical case study focused around a conundrum that remains appropriate for discussing health care stewardship in the twenty-first century.

Hardin begins to explain the reasons behind the initial development of the tragedy of the commons. Imagine a pasture accessible to everyone in a clearly defined geographic area. It is expected that each herdsman will try to keep as many cattle as possible on the pasture, known as the "commons." This arrangement may work reasonably well for centuries because tribal wars, poaching, and disease keep the numbers of both people and livestock well below the land's carrying capacity. Eventually, however, the day of reckoning arrives—the day when the long-desired goal of social stability becomes a reality. At this point, the inherent logic of the commons inevitably leads to tragedy.

Assuming the herdsmen are acting rationally, each herdsman seeks to maximize his gain. Consciously or unconsciously, they ask themselves, "What is the benefit to me of adding one more animal to my herd on the commons?"

This benefit has both a positive and a negative component. The positive component comes from the incremental addition of one animal to the commons. Since the herdsman receives all the proceeds from the sale of the additional animal, the positive benefit is nearly +1. The negative component results from the additional overgrazing caused by adding one more animal to the commons. Since the effects of overgrazing are shared by all herdsmen, the negative impact on any individual herdsman is only a fraction of -1. When combining these partial utilities, the rational herdsman concludes that the only sensible course of action is to add another animal to his herd growing in number on the commons. And then another; and yet another. However, this conclusion is reached by every rational herdsman sharing the commons. This is where the tragedy lies.

Each man is locked into a system that compels him to increase his herd without limit—in a world that is limited at best. Hardin (1968) concludes the "ruin" is the destination toward which all men rush, each pursuing his own best interest in a society that believes in the freedom of the commons. Freedom in a common brings ruin to all.

In 1975, Dr. Howard H. Hiatt, an American biomedical scientist and one of the discoverers of mRNA, advanced the conversation about the tragedy of the commons by connecting it to the management of finite healthcare resources. He highlighted the tragedy of the healthcare commons, emphasizing the challenges in balancing limited resources within the US healthcare delivery system. Hiatt suggested that the total resources available for medical care are analogous to the grazing area in Hardin's commons, while the medical practices utilizing those resources are similar to Hardin's grazing animals.

Dr. Hiatt observed that no one would dispute the existence of a limit to the resources any society can allocate to medical care, and by 1975, it was widely acknowledged that society was rapidly nearing this limit. He also pointed out that a significant portion of the increasing demands on healthcare resources was aimed at addressing the inadequacies of medical care for large segments of the population. In discussing the challenges of overpopulation and finite energy resources, Hiatt posed the critical question: How can we prevent the additional strain on the medical commons from leading to societal ruin?

7.2 PROTECTING THE MEDICAL COMMONS

All stakeholders in the U.S. healthcare delivery system stretch the medical commons to its limits due to competing interests. The absence of real-time clinical data from the point of care has resulted in inadequate prioritization for establishing effective public policy. The high prevalence of chronic conditions, both in the U.S. and globally, significantly impacts the allocation of healthcare resources needed to manage these patients. This narrow focus on individual patients diverts attention from the broader needs of the U.S. population.

As it stands, the marginal benefits gained for individual patients can jeopardize the overall health, wellness, and well-being of the entire US population. Unrestricted access to the medical commons has led to the imprudent use of scarce healthcare resources, which serves neither individuals nor society effectively. Evidence-based medicine and clinical practice guidelines, derived from randomized controlled trials, have prompted organized medicine to move away from practices that fall into this category.

The health, wellness, and well-being of the general public have traditionally been the focus of healthcare delivery systems at all levels of organization, from individual patient care in the doctor's office to global population health management. However, competing interests between the concept of salutogenesis and models of health vs. the concept of pathogenesis and models of care. Regardless, this has ultimately led to the overuse of the medical commons, leading to a more expansive and intricate practice of modern medicine, locally to globally.

Dr. Hiatt, recognizing the potential consequences of overusing the medical commons, posed the question: "Who will protect the medical commons?" At the turn of the twentieth century, Hiatt observed that the medical commons featured relatively few expressive clinical practices, lacked well-defined limits on the use of resources, and relied on conscientious practitioners and the cottage-like industry of medicine at that time to draw only what was necessary and essential for patient care.

By the twenty-first century, the U.S. healthcare delivery system had undergone several transformations, culminating in today's chronic condition model of care. In addition, US healthcare delivery has become increasingly subordinate to and influenced by the U.S. medical-industrial complex. Complex factors have expanded the boundaries of the medical commons, posing major existential threats to public health both nationally and globally. These threats include Anthropocene climate change and rising greenhouse gas emissions, increasing natural disasters, global pandemics (e.g., COVID-19), institutional bias and racism, economic inequities and widening health disparities, an aging population, re-emerging infectious diseases, and a sharp rise in chronic health conditions such as diabetes, cardiovascular disease, and neurodegenerative disorders.

Keeping the focus on protecting the medical commons, many questions develop to help avert a major tragedy including:

1. How should priorities be set in the United States?
2. Who should set these priorities?

3. How much should be allocated for health care resources?

4. Of the total medical commons, how much should be allocated for:

    a. Medical care?

    b. Basic science?

    c. Medical education?

    d. Public health?

    e. Medical research?

5. If a disease management program receives a limited sum of funding, how should that money be optimally used?

6. Who should qualify for treatment of their chronic end-stage diseases (e.g., end-stage renal disease and dialysis)?

7. Of all the stakeholders in the US health care delivery system, who should make health care resource allocation decisions? The government? The medical-industrial complex?

8. On what basis should health care resource allocation decisions be made?

Hiatt (1975) identified issues related to the commons that remain relevant to the current state of healthcare delivery. First, he recognized that health prevention and health promotion offered the greatest long-term opportunities for protecting the resources of the medical commons. Second, he urged all clinicians to counsel and encourage the public to understand more about their individual health, wellness, and well-being. Understanding the limitations and uncertainties of medical care, Hiatt believed, society would make decisions regarding health care resource utilization on a fully informed basis if they understood how important it was to remain healthy. Lastly, Dr. Hiatt believed it was essential that the process of decision-making with respect to the medical commons be maximally flexible. The passage of time in healthcare delivery generates insights into what is effective and what is not across all levels of organization, from sub-molecular and cellular to the biosphere. To use the medical commons wisely and respectfully, process improvement must be continuously reviewed and revised.

7.3 MANAGING LIMITED MEDICAL RESOURCES IN THE 21ST CENTURY

Unfortunately, the issues related to the medical commons that Hiatt so eloquently identified in 1975 remain unresolved within the American healthcare delivery system today. Market-based attempts to control health care resource utilization by instituting the principles and practices of managed care and utilization management did nothing to limit the irresponsible use of health care resources by all the healthcare stakeholders. In fact, it is common knowledge that the U.S. spends more per capita on health care than any other developed or developing nation without achieving the highest quality, safety, and outcomes for the patients served (OECD, 2023).

Managing health care resources today is really a question of cost-efficiency vs. quality of care and patient safety. All stakeholders in the U.S. healthcare delivery system are interested in efficiency, but it is the clinicians who struggle with their ongoing role in managing the appropriate use of health care resources. This struggle remains deeply rooted in medical ethics (Cassel and Brennan 2007).

As previously mentioned, the traditional core value of medicine is the primacy of the patient's well-being over the self-interest of the clinician and implicitly over other social concerns as well (Cassel et al., 2007). This is highly desirable when very ill patients seek medical attention from an expert clinician. There is a fundamental inequality in the fund of knowledge and power between the clinician and patient. In dire situations, patients acquiesce to the clinical expertise of the clinician whom they believe has their best interests at heart.

Should the clinician be concerned about, as well as committed to, managing the medical resources (i.e., medical commons) for his or her patients? The answer is yes. Today, it is impossible to avoid the fact that clinicians live and work in a medical commons and bear responsibility for making resource decisions that directly affect its utilization (Cassel et al., 2007). However, according to Starr (1982), the allopathic medical community worked aggressively to assert its control over the U.S. healthcare delivery system by partnering with the US medical-industrial complex and further widening the affiliation between itself and public health sectors, while championing fee-for-service payment.

A basic appreciation for the medical commons escapes many clinicians today. Healthcare resource utilization, both directly and indirectly, benefit patients in need of health care goods and services. The implementation of the managed care model introduced into the US healthcare delivery system in the 1980s fostered this attitude (Daniels 1986). In fact, it became widely understood within the allopathic medical community that any savings from market-based activities would likely be used either to reduce the deficit in government-funded programs (e.g., Medicare and Medicaid) or to enhance the profit margins of the medical-industrial complex (e.g., PHARMA). Clinicians faced ethical and moral challenges with the rationing of the medical commons at the point of care, known as bedside rationing, because it compromised the sacred clinician-patient relationship and associated clinicians with cost-control measures aimed at benefiting payers' business interests rather than improving patient care.

To date, clinicians have largely relinquished responsibility for the medical commons in the United States to two major forces: market-based dynamics and government regulation. Can either of these forces effectively manage the medical commons without clinician involvement? The delivery of medical care and the essential public health services over the past 50 years suggests strongly the answer would be no.

Government regulation, particularly with regard to the Medicare system at the federal level, has significantly contributed to the irresponsible use of limited healthcare resources within the U.S. healthcare delivery system. The oversight of physician service costs, based on the now-defunct (replaced in 2015 by MACRA) annual Medicare Sustainable Growth Rate (SGR) calculations, illustrated this issue year over year.

Each winter, lobbyists from major professional medical organizations worked to prevent reductions in Medicare rates resulting from the Centers for Medicare and Medicaid Services (CMS) calculations of clinical services provided and their associated costs (Plested, 2006).

In 2015, MACRA (Medicare Access and CHIP Reauthorization Act) replaced the Medicare's SGR (Steinbrook, 2015). The intention of MACRA was clearly to manage health care resource utilization and control costs. However, this strategy has failed on both accords. The momentum for payment reform and the specific payment mechanisms notwithstanding, physicians are likely to advocate for Medicare payment updates that at least keep up with inflation and the cost of living. At some point, the cumulative effect of the new payment updates will not keep up with physician costs, unless the volume and cost of services substantially decrease, which is the same underlying issue as with the old payment updates under the SGR process. Each physician continues to act like the herdsman on the commons trying to maximize his own personal happiness (Cassel and Brennan 2007).

Market dynamics create a comparable "moral-agency" dilemma between physicians and the commercial health insurance industry. The managed care experiment (i.e., Health Maintenance Organizations-HMOs) from the 1980's led to physicians' mistrust regarding where healthcare savings from cost-control measures are directed and the significance of profit margins within the industry (Cassel and Brennan 2007). The lack of transparency, accountability, and truthfulness on the part of US health insurance companies created the perfect storm for a major paradigm shift towards value-based models of care (e.g., patient-centered medical homes and accountable care organizations) in the 1990's.

Renewing the medical commons can strengthen clinician accountability without undermining the quality of medical services at the point of care (Cassel and Brennan 2007). Today, consumer-directed medical care and efforts to increase transparency and accountability about quality, access, cost and appropriate use of health care services enables patients to make informed decisions about their medical care. This should result in the better use of today's limited health care resources without compromising the positive health outcomes related to the care provided. For the most part, clinicians today do not have a sense of responsibility for health care resource utilization, nor do they feel as if they have any influence over health care resource use within the US health care delivery system.

Are there examples that exist in the US healthcare delivery system today advanced as models of ethically and empirically-driven health care stewardship? Holistic, integrated and comprehensive healthcare delivery systems that provide some of the necessary organizational structures and processes that can bring transparency, accountability, and truthfulness back to all healthcare stakeholders can renew the medical commons (Nasiri et al, 2019). For example, a group practice accepts the notion of group responsibility. All the physicians within the group practice accept responsibility for the overall health, wellness, and well-being of every patient within the population the practice serves. This dual responsibility for a population and the individual patient compels the clinicians within the practice to be accountable for quality care, patient safety, trust and truthfulness, cost efficiency, and accessibility (Enthoven and Tollen 2004). Multispecialty group practice supported with proper incentives offers the coordination of chronic and complex disease management infrastructure to support the use of evidence-based medical care, and the ability to afford, invest in, and implement clinical information technology (Crosson 2004; Nasiri et al, 2019). Again, all is done in the name of transparency and accountability for quality care, accessibility, and cost efficiency within the context of using the medical commons responsibly.

7.4 THE PATIENT-CENTERED MEDICAL HOME

One example of managing the medical commons with a major paradigm shift to a multi-level organizational structure and process change is the establishment of the primary medical home for individual patients and populations (AHRQ, 2019; NCQA, 2020). First access to care, coordination of care, longitudinal care, and comprehensive care are just a few of the attributes that the primary medical home will provide that allows for health care stewardship to flourish within today's US health care delivery system.

The Patient-Centered Medical Home (PCMH) (AHRQ, 2019; NCQA, 2020) is a model of care delivery designed to improve patient outcomes by providing comprehensive, patient-centered, and coordinated care. At its core, the PCMH emphasizes the use of primary medical care as the central hub for patient care management, ensuring that all aspects of a patient's health, wellness, and well-being are addressed cohesively and efficiently. This approach is structured around five foundational functions and attributes including comprehensive care, patient-centered care, coordinated care, accessible services, and quality/safety of care.

Comprehensive care within the PCMH model involves a team-based approach to healthcare delivery, where a primary care physician leads a group of healthcare professionals to meet the majority of a patient's physical and mental health care needs. This team may include physicians, nurse practitioners, nurses, pharmacists, nutritionists, social workers, and other professionals. By offering a broad spectrum of services, the PCMH aims to provide holistic care that addresses proactive care, acute illness and injury care, and chronic condition care.

Patient-centered care is a hallmark of the PCMH, emphasizing the importance of understanding and respecting each patient's unique culture, preferences, needs and values. This attribute encourages an active partnership between patients and their healthcare providers, fostering an agency where individuals and their families are empowered to take a participatory role in their own medical care. The over-arching goal is to create a healthcare experience that is personalized and responsive to individual patient preferences, needs, and values, thus enhancing patient satisfaction and engagement.

Coordinated care in the PCMH model ensures that medical care is organized across all elements of the broader healthcare delivery system, including specialty care, hospitals, home health care, and community services. This function is crucial for preventing fragmentation of care, which can lead to process errors, inefficiencies, and poorer health outcomes. By maintaining clear communication channels and using interoperable health information systems and technology, the PCMH facilitates seamless transitions of care with seamless continuity across different settings and providers.

Accessibility is another foundational aspect of the PCMH, which strives to make healthcare services more accessible by reducing obstacles and barriers to care. This may include offering extended office hours, providing easier scheduling options, and using telehealth services and broad-band technology to outreach to a subset of patients who may have difficulty accessing traditional in-person office visits. Enhancing access to care is fundamental to improving overall health outcomes and ensuring that patients receive timely and appropriate medical care.

Finally, the PCMH model places a strong emphasis on quality and safety, continually monitoring and improving healthcare practices to achieve the best possible patient outcomes. This involves the use of empirically-driven, evidence-based medicine, clinical decision-support tools, performance measurement, and quality improvement initiatives. By focusing on quality and safety, the PCMH aims to provide high-value care that is both effective and efficient, ultimately leading to better health outcomes and reduced healthcare costs (AHRQ, 2019; NCQA, 2020).

7.5 MACROECONOMICS IMPACT ON HEALTHCARE STEWARDSHIP

Macroeconomics significantly impacts healthcare stewardship by influencing the availability and allocation of resources within the healthcare system (Saltman et al., 2000). Economic growth, for instance, affects government revenues and, consequently, public spending on healthcare. In periods of economic prosperity, governments typically have more funds to allocate toward healthcare infrastructure, technology, and services, enhancing overall healthcare quality and access. Conversely, during economic downturns, budget cuts and resource constraints can lead to reduced funding for healthcare, negatively affecting service delivery, staffing, and the availability of medical supplies.

Inflation, a foundational macroeconomic variable, also plays a critical role in healthcare stewardship. Rising inflation increases the cost of medical supplies, pharmaceuticals, and healthcare services. This can strain healthcare budgets, especially in open, complex, and adaptive healthcare systems reliant on fixed budgets or insurance reimbursements. High inflation rates can force healthcare providers to make difficult choices, such as reducing services or delaying investments in new technology and refreshed facilities, ultimately impacting patient quality of medical care and positive health outcomes. Additionally, inflation can erode the purchasing power of individuals, making healthcare less affordable for many and potentially increasing the number of uninsured or underinsured individuals.

Unemployment rates, another macroeconomic factor, influence healthcare stewardship by affecting insurance coverage and health outcomes. High unemployment often leads to a loss of employer-sponsored health insurance, increasing the reliance on essential public health services or leading to gaps in medical coverage. This shift can strain local and state public health systems and reduce access to proactive care, acute illness and injury care, and chronic condition care and services. Moreover, unemployment is associated with higher levels of stress overload and untreated diseases of despair (e.g., depression, anxiety, and suicidal ideation) increasing the demand for healthcare services at a time when resources may be more limited.

Financial exchange rates and international trade policies also impact healthcare stewardship by affecting the cost and availability of imported medical supplies, equipment, and pharmaceuticals. Fluctuations in international exchange rates can lead to increased costs for imported goods, affecting the financial sustainability of healthcare providers. Trade policies that impose tariffs or restrictions on medical goods can further complicate medical supply chains, leading to shortages and higher costs for essential healthcare-related items. These economic factors necessitate careful management and strategic planning by healthcare leaders to ensure that high-quality care remains accessible and affordable, despite the significant external economic pressures.

7.6 MICROECONOMICS IMPACT ON HEALTHCARE STEWARDSHIP

Microeconomics profoundly impacts healthcare stewardship through the dynamics of supply and demand, pricing, and the behavior of individual healthcare providers and consumers (Costa-Font et al., 2020). The principles of supply and demand determine the availability and cost of healthcare services. For instance, in areas with a high concentration of healthcare providers, competition can drive down prices and improve service quality, benefiting patients. Conversely, in regions with limited healthcare resources, providers may have greater pricing power, leading to higher costs and potentially reduced access to care. Understanding these market dynamics is essential for healthcare stewards to ensure resources are allocated efficiently and equitably.

Pricing strategies in healthcare are another critical aspect of microeconomics that affects stewardship. Healthcare providers must balance the need to cover costs and generate sufficient revenue with the goal of making services affordable for patients. This involves making decisions about pricing for different services, negotiating reimbursement rates with insurers, and managing costs. Effective pricing strategies can ensure that healthcare organizations remain financially viable while providing high-quality care. However, pricing that is too high can limit access for patients, particularly those without sufficient insurance coverage or financial resources, highlighting the need for careful and ethical pricing decisions in healthcare stewardship.

The behavior of individual healthcare providers and patients also shapes the microeconomic landscape of healthcare. Providers make decisions about the allocation of their time and resources, which impacts the availability and quality of care delivered. For example, the decision to adopt new medical technologies or new clinical practice guidelines may improve patient outcomes but also involves significant upfront investment and potential downside-risk. On the patient side, decisions about when and where to seek care, adherence to treatment plans, and willingness to pay for services affect demand and utilization patterns. Healthcare stewards must understand these behaviors to design interventions and healthy public policies that align incentives with desired health outcomes, ensuring that resources are used effectively and efficiently.

Market structures and competition within the healthcare sector further influence microeconomic outcomes and stewardship. In monopolistic or oligopolistic markets, a few providers may dominate, potentially leading to higher prices and less innovation. Conversely, in more competitive markets, the pressure to attract and retain patients can significantly drive improvements in service quality and efficiency. Healthcare stewards must navigate these market structures, advocating for healthy public policies that encourage friendly competition and eliminate anti-competitive practices. By fostering a competitive yet collaborative environment, stewards can help ensure that healthcare systems deliver high-quality, accessible, and affordable care to all patients.

7.7 THE HEALTHCARE MARKETPLACE

Since the time of Adam Smith, the majority of economists have advocated the use of free markets as a mechanism of promoting efficiency (Bassiry et al., 1993). Smith himself theorized that in a free market society, individuals of their own volition pursue their own self-interests. In doing so, these independent individuals will be led to produce an allocation of resources that maximizes society's utility. There are certain conditions that require free markets to exercise efficient resource allocation. Above all, the first condition is *perfect competition*. This means that a market exists in which no individual buyer or seller can affect the price by his or her own actions. Without this condition, market distortions occur resulting in inefficient allocations of resources.

The contemporary Adam Smith's free market for health care efficiency contains many distortions, including the asymmetry of information between clinicians and patients, the clinician's dual role as patient advocate and independent business owner, the effect of insurance in reducing the apparent cost of health care goods and services to patients (the full cost of health care is not charged to patients, aka "price-wedge" distortion), tax subsidies that have a similar effect on consumers' decisions to purchase insurance, and monopoly power bestowed on certain professions and in some countries, health insurance plans, thereby limiting competition.

According to Wells et al. (2007), there were three classic efforts to describe, quantify, and propose solutions to the free market distortions in health care delivery: the Medical Commons, the Rand Health Insurance Experiment, and the Consumer Choice Health Plan.

Discussed at length earlier in this chapter, Hiatt (1975) challenged the medical profession to establish who was responsible for protecting the *medical commons*. Hiatt referred to an article by Harden (1968) in which he used the analogy between the practice of medicine and the practice of a group of herdsmen whose cattle share a common pasture to describe two important health care market distortions: the *price wedge* and *asymmetry of information*. Keeping the number of animals small in relation to the capacity of the pasture allows each herdsman to increase his holdings without detriment to the general welfare. However, when the pasture reaches near capacity, each animal has the potential to do irrevocable harm to the long-term sustainability of the system through overconsumption. Hiatt argued that the medical commons was fast approaching depletion as a consequence of free access to health care goods and services resulting in overconsumption (i.e., moral hazard) and increasing costs exacerbated by rapidly expanding, expensive technology of unproven effectiveness.

Hiatt (1975) proposed three types of solutions to this lack of health care stewardship: clinical evaluation of current medical practices (i.e., evidence-based medicine), setting a national health agenda, and expanding health care to include the social determinants of health with a focus on proactive health prevention, promotion, and protection.

The second classic effort to describe, quantify, and propose solutions to the free market distortions in health care delivery was a study performed by the Rand Corporation entitled, the Rand Health Insurance Experiment (aka, HIE). This experiment was one of the largest randomized social trials of its kind and occurred during the 1970s. The study asked three basic questions: How do demand-side incentives (e.g., cost-sharing) affect total health care utilization and expenditures? What is the effect of cost-sharing on individual health status? What are the consequences of cost-sharing on appropriateness and quality of care? The first two questions address the effect of the *price-wedge* distortion on expenditures and health and the last question partially addresses the asymmetry of information (Wells et al. 2007).

The HIE enrolled 7700 adults less than sixty-five years of age in six sites (both urban and rural) across the United States. Study participants were randomly assigned to one of five groups:

1. Free medical care
2. 25 percent cost-sharing up to a maximum amount
3. 50 percent cost-sharing up to a maximum amount
4. 95 percent cost-sharing up to a maximum amount
5. Enrollment in a nonprofit health maintenance organization

All participants enrolled in the study were observed for a period of three to five years.

The effects of cost sharing on total expenditures were significant. Patients with a 25 percent coinsurance spent 20 percent less than those with free medical care, and those with 95 percent coinsurance spent approximately 30 percent less (Newhouse et al. 1981). Savings resulted from using fewer health care services rather than from finding health care providers with lower prices. As individual financial responsibility for health care increased by creating a self-imposed restriction on utilization of healthcare resources.

There was no significant difference in overall individual health status between study participants who enrolled in free medical care and cost-sharing insurance plans (Brook et al. 1983). Families that used medical resources more frequently because of less out-of-pocket costs gained no significant observed advantage in terms of their own individual health improvement. Smoking status, cholesterol level, and weight did not differ as a function of insurance plan. There was one significant change among the poorest and sickest 6 percent of the sample. Free medical care was associated with better health specifically related to diastolic blood pressure, functional far vision, and risk of dying. Increased physician visits by those families in the free medical care group resulted in the positive health care outcomes.

The effect of cost-sharing on appropriateness of care revealed that cost-sharing reduced overall medical care utilization. However, there was no significant difference in change of use between effective and ineffective care (Lohr et al. 1986). Restriction of health care as a result of facing a higher *true cost* did not result in patients increasing the proportion of their medical care considered appropriate by the Rand experts or conversely, decreasing the proportion considered inappropriate. Siu et al. (1986) reported no statistically significant differences in inappropriate hospital admissions between cost-sharing plans. According to Wells et al. (2007), these published findings from the Rand Corporation Health Insurance Experiment may have influenced the trend in health care delivery to focus on supply-sided instruments to improve on appropriateness and quality of care (i.e., evidence-based medicine, clinical practice guidelines).

Enthoven (1978) studied and reported the third and final classic effort to describe, quantify, and propose solutions to free market distortions in health care. Enthoven developed a proposal for a new national health insurance system known as the Consumer Choice Health Plan (CCHP). This proposal involved controlling costs through direct competition by health insurance plans for enrollees. The plans would be required to do the following: offer a clear, understandable, and detailed breakdown of enrollment costs and covered benefits to all individuals, permit individuals to compare plans allowing for informed purchasing decisions, and encourage competitively priced coverage.

A separate provision existed for eliminating the existing system of tax incentives for health insurance. Federal-state partnerships would offer subsidies so that individuals could buy health insurance coverage. In order to control cost escalation, provisions existed for tax credits to individuals who purchased efficient health insurance plans. These tax credits would allow individuals to keep the savings generated from choosing a less costly health insurance plan. To ensure equity between rich and poor, another provision existed for vouchers to help lower-income individuals and families participate. To prevent plans from limiting enrollment to individuals from whom they are more likely to profit, the CCHP included rules such as open enrollment (i.e., no age, gender, or preexisting health condition exclusions) and flat premiums based on market-area actuarial costs (i.e., community rating).

Unfortunately, Enthoven's CCHP proposal failed because it would have been difficult to reverse existing tax incentives in place at the time of the initial proposal. However, parts of this proposal became the catalyst for a managed competition movement found in the 1994 Clinton health plan proposal.

7.8 21ST CENTURY HEALTHCARE MARKET FORCES

According to Wells et al. (2007), in the early 2000's, US healthcare policy initiatives to reduce health care market distortions focused on both the supply and demand side of the health care marketplace. Pay-for-performance (P4P) encouraged the symmetry of information between patients and clinicians. Health plans, both public and private, offered to clinicians and health care institutions additional reimbursement for the delivery of high quality and appropriate medical services. This process ensured that patients receive important medical care that was not sufficiently prioritized before this process was initiated (Rosenthal and Dudley 2007).

Another solution for free market distortion takes aim at *price-wedge* distortions. Consumer-directed health care (CDHC) plans are in reality a variation of the catastrophic health insurance plans of the twentieth century or the 95 percent cost-sharing intervention group within the Rand Corporation Health Insurance Experiment. The CDHC plans attack price-wedge distortions by offering less expensive premiums in combination with high deductibles. This ultimately places responsibility back with individual patients to decide which health care goods and services to purchase. However, CDHC plans did not meet equitable criteria because these plans tend to favor children and healthy individuals while women and sick individuals face escalating health care costs (Woolhandler and Himmelstein 2007).

In 2007, a report surfaced in the medical literature describing a value-based insurance design (Fendrick and Chernew 2007). This design was a variation of the CDHC plan differentiating between health care services that are effective and cost-efficient and those that are not. These plans would cover both effective and cost-efficient services with a lower deductible thus reserving a high deductible for the "less desirable" interventions. Value-based insurance design attempted to fix both the *price-wedge* and *asymmetry of information* distortions. It resembled a health care goods and services formulary that would likely require significant administrative overhead to manage. (Oberlander et al. 2001).

Few employer-sponsored health care plans in the United States used value-based purchasing strategies that include incentives and programs aimed at improving the quality and performance of medical care for enrollees (Rosenthal et al. 2007). According to Wells et al. (2007), it was time for all the stakeholders of the US health care delivery system to admit that it was impossible to develop healthy public policy initiatives that can correct market distortions and produce an efficient health care marketplace. A truly efficient health care marketplace is one in which value received per dollar spent is maximized and the distribution of health care services is both fair and equitable for the population as a whole (Porter, 2021). Unfortunately, for the US health care delivery system, both the political system and the social consensus was not clear about whether every person in society has a right to health care regardless of their ability to pay.

Fast forward to 2024. The healthcare marketplace is influenced by several key forces that significantly impact healthcare stewardship. One of the primary drivers is the shifting payer landscape. The profitability of government segments, particularly Medicare Advantage, is projected to outpace that of commercial segments. This shift is driven by increased Medicare Advantage penetration and a growing dual-eligible population, despite regulatory pressures and economic uncertainties affecting Medicaid enrollment (Patel and Singhal, 2024; Rao, 2024).

Economic conditions, such as inflation and recession risks, also play a critical role. While inflation is projected to decrease, ongoing financial pressures compel healthcare organizations to focus on cost containment and efficiency improvements. This includes increased outsourcing of administrative functions and leveraging technology for better operational management (Patel and Singhal, 2024; Corpart, 2024). Labor shortages and wage inflation continue to challenge healthcare systems, necessitating innovations in workforce management and the adoption of digital health solutions to maintain service levels and financial stability (Rao, 2024; Corpart, 2024) Pharmacy sector dynamics, including regulatory changes and the evolution of specialty pharmacies, are also significant. The specialty pharmacy segment is experiencing rapid growth due to high utilization and the introduction of advanced therapies. However, this growth is tempered by reimbursement pressures and the need for increased transparency in drug pricing under new legislative frameworks like the Inflation Reduction Act of 2022 (Rao, 2024).

Additionally, the healthcare market is seeing a rise in private equity involvement, with strategic acquisitions and public-to-private deals becoming more common. This trend is facilitated by lower valuations and the strategic need for healthcare organizations to diversify and enhance their capabilities amid financial constraints (Rao, 2024).

Overall, these marketplace forces require healthcare stewards to navigate a complex environment of economic pressures, regulatory changes, and technological advancements, all while striving to improve care quality and maintain financial health.

Professional responsibilities for the medical commons are inherent within the clinician-patient interaction. The clinical care for patients diminishes when there are insufficient health care resources for use by all patients. Rising health care costs threaten the care of many by increasing the number of uninsured patients, thus restricting access to the current formal U.S. health care delivery system. Inappropriate utilization and waste of the finite health care resources abounds. The ethical challenges of managing the medical commons require clinicians to link clinical care to cost of care.

Market-based and regulatory approaches place the welfare of patients in the hands of people other than their clinicians. The distribution of health care resources today occurs without regard for the caring, commitment, clinical acumen, and wisdom of experienced clinicians. Clinicians will be required to make an active decision about the approach they will take both individually and collectively regarding health care stewardship activities. It is apparent that clinician engagement in the medical commons, along with the engagement of all the stakeholders of the U.S. health care delivery system is the only approach that will ensure proper and appropriate allocation of health care resources leading to improved health care outcomes.

7.9 THE IMPACT OF POLICY ON HEALTH ECONOMICS AND HEALTHCARE STEWARDSHIP

Healthy public policies play a critical role in shaping the landscape of health economics, influencing how resources are distributed, healthcare services are delivered, and health outcomes are achieved. For example, policies that expand health insurance coverage, such as the Affordable Care Act (ACA) in the United States, aim to increase access to healthcare and reduce financial barriers for individuals (Maruthappu et al., 2013). These policies can lead to broader population health improvements, but they also have significant economic implications, including changes in healthcare spending, insurance premiums, and the financial performance of healthcare providers. Additionally, policies that promote cost-containment measures, such as value-based care and bundled payments, aim to improve the efficiency of healthcare delivery by incentivizing providers to focus on quality rather than quantity of care. The impact of these policies is assessed through economic evaluations, which help determine their effectiveness in improving health outcomes relative to their costs (Jones, 2018).

Healthcare stewardship is heavily influenced by policies that govern the management and allocation of health resources (Turner et al., 2021). Policies that establish regulatory frameworks ensure that healthcare providers adhere to standards that promote patient safety, quality of care, and ethical practices. For instance, policies mandating transparency in healthcare pricing can empower consumers to make more informed decisions, potentially driving competition and reducing costs. Policies that support public health initiatives, such as vaccination programs and tobacco control measures, are essential components of stewardship, aiming to prevent disease and promote health at the population level. Furthermore, policies that invest in health information technology can enhance the efficiency and coordination of care by improving data sharing and communication among providers. Effective stewardship policies also focus on workforce development, ensuring that there are sufficient and appropriately trained healthcare professionals to meet the needs of the population. By guiding the strategic allocation of resources and setting priorities, policies help stewards create sustainable healthcare systems that are capable of adapting to emerging challenges and opportunities.

7.10 HOW DO HEALTHY PUBLIC POLICIES AFFECT HEALTHCARE STEWARDSHIP?

Healthy public policies are essential for guiding the planning, development, and implementation of healthcare services and systems. Here are several examples of healthy public policies from different areas of healthcare.

1. Public Health Policies.

    a. Vaccination Policies: Mandating vaccinations for children and adults to prevent the spread of infectious diseases, such as measles, mumps, and influenza.

    b. Smoking Bans: Implementing bans on smoking in public places to reduce exposure to secondhand smoke and lower the incidence of smoking-related diseases.

2. Health Coverage and Insurance.

    a. Universal Health Coverage: Policies aimed at providing health insurance to all citizens, such as the National Health Service (NHS) in the UK or the Affordable Care Act (ACA) in the United States.

    b. Medicaid and Medicare: Government-funded programs in the United States that provide health coverage to the aged, disabled, blind, and low-income individuals (Medicaid) and those aged 65 and older (Medicare).

3. Health Equity Policies.

    a. Reducing Health Disparities: Initiatives to address social determinants of health, such as housing, education, and income, to reduce health disparities among different populations.

    b. Cultural Humility Training: Requiring healthcare providers to undergo training in cultural humility to improve care for diverse populations considering their cultural preferences, needs, and values with respect and empathy.

4. Environmental Health Policies

    a. Clean Air Act: Legislation aimed at reducing air pollution to improve public health by setting limits on emissions from industries and vehicles.

    b. Water Quality Standards: Regulations ensuring safe drinking water by setting limits on contaminants and requiring regular testing and reporting.

5. Proactive Health Policies.

    a. Routine Screenings: Guidelines recommending regular screenings for conditions like cancer, diabetes, and hypertension to detect and treat diseases early.

    b. Nutritional Guidelines: Policies promoting healthy eating, such as dietary guidelines and food labeling requirements, to combat obesity and related health issues.

6. Healthcare Quality and Safety.

    a. Patient Safety Regulations: Policies mandating practices to reduce medical errors, such as surgical checklists and infection control protocols.

    b. Accreditation and Certification: Requiring healthcare facilities to obtain accreditation from recognized bodies to ensure they meet certain quality and safety standards.

7. Mental Health Policies.

    a. Mental Health Parity: Laws requiring health insurance plans to provide equal coverage for mental health and substance use disorders as for physical health conditions.

    b. Community Mental Health Services: Policies promoting the development and funding of community-based mental health services to improve access and reduce stigma. E.g.,

Mobile Response and Stabilization Services, Emergency Departments exclusively for acute psychiatric conditions

8. Pharmaceutical and Drug Policies.

   a. Drug Approval Processes: Regulations governing the approval of new drugs to ensure they are safe, efficacious and effective before reaching the market.

   b. Prescription Drug Monitoring Programs (PDMPs): most if not all states have their own systems to track the prescribing and dispensing of controlled substances to combat opioid misuse and abuse.

   c. Price containment for vulnerable and marginalized Americans so they don't have to choose between their life-saving medication and housing or food.

9. Global Health Policies.

   a. International Health Regulations (IHR): A legally binding framework for countries to prevent and respond to public health risks that have the potential to cross borders.

   b. Global Health Security Agenda (GHSA): An international effort to strengthen the world's ability to prevent, detect, and respond to infectious disease threats.

10. Health Information Technology.

   a. Electronic Health Records (EHR) Incentives: Policies providing financial incentives for healthcare providers to adopt and meaningfully use EHRs and data platforms (e.g., population health and SDOH platforms integrated with EHRs) to improve patient care.

   b. Telehealth Regulations: Guidelines and policies promoting the use of telehealth services to increase access to care, especially in rural and underserved areas.

These examples illustrate the broad scope of healthy public policies and their critical role in shaping healthcare systems, improving public health outcomes, and exercising transparent and accountable healthcare stewardship.

7.11 REFERENCES

Agency for Healthcare Research and Quality. (2019). Patient-Centered Medical Home Resource Center. Retrieved from https://pcmh. ahrq.gov.

Bassiry, G. R., Jones, M. (1993) Adam Smith and the ethics of contemporary capitalism.*Journal of Business Ethics*12: 621-627.

Brook, R. H., Ware Jr., J.E., Rogers, W.H., et al. (1983) Does free care improve adults' health? Results from a randomized controlled trial. *N Engl J Med* 309 (23): 1426–1434.

Cassel, C. K., Brennan, T.E. (2007) Managing medical resources: Return to the commons? *JAMA* 297 (22): 2518–2521.

Corpart, G. (2024). The Face of Healthcare in 2024. Global Health Intelligence. Accessed at https://globalhealthintelligence.com/ ghi-analysis/the-face-of-healthca re-i n-2024/.

Costa-Font, J., Turati, G., Batinti, A. (2020)The political economy of health and healthcare: The rise of the patient citizen. Cambridge University Press.

Crosson, J. (2004) Panelist for: Delivery systems matter! Improving quality and efficiency in health care (transcript). Kaiser Permanente Institute for Health Policy and Health Affairs 1-Day conference, March 17, 2004. Washington DC. http://www.kaisernetwork. org/health_cast/uploaded_files/031704_kp_iom.pdf. Accessed October 31, 2007.

Daniels, N. (1986) Why saying no to patients in the United States is so hard: Cost containment, justice, and provider autonomy. *N Engl J Med* 314: 1380–1383.

Enthoven, A. C. (1978) Consumer-choice health plan, II: A national-health-insurance proposal based on regulated competition in the private sector. *N Engl J Med* 298 (13): 709–720.

Enthoven, A. C., Tollen, L.A. (2004) *Toward a 21st century health system: The contributions and promise of a prepaid group practice.* San Francisco, California: Jossey-Bass.

Fendrick, A. M., Chernew, M.A. (2007) Value-based insurance design: A "clinically sensitive, fiscally responsible" approach to mitigate the adverse clinical effects of high -deductible consumer-directed health plans. *J Gen Intern Med* 22 (6): 890–891.

Hardin, G. (1968) The tragedy of the commons. *Science* 168; 162: 1243–1248.

Hiatt, H. H. (1975) Protecting the medical commons: Who is responsible? *N Engl J Med* 293: 235–241.

Jones, L. K. (2016) The roadmap to value-based care.*JAMA Neurology* 73 (10): 1173-1174.

Lohr, K. N., R. H. Brook, Kamberg, C.J., et al. (1986) Effect of cost-sharing on use of medically effective and less effective care. *Med Care* 24 (9): S31–S38.

Maruthappu, M., Ologunde, R., Gunarajasingam, A. (2013) Is health care a right? Health reforms in the USA and their impact upon the concept of care.*Annals of Medicine and Surgery*2 (1): 15-17.

Nasiri, T., A. Takian, Yazdani. S. (2019) Stewardship in Health, Designing a Multi-Layer Meta Model: A Review Article.*Iranian Journal of Public Health*48 (4): 579–592.

National Committee for Quality Assurance. (2020). NCQA Patient-Centered Medical Home (PCMH). Retrieved from https://www.ncqa.org/programs /health-care-providers-practices / patient-centered-medical-home-pcmh/.

Newhouse, J. P. (1993) Insurance Experiment Group. *Free for all? Lessons from the RAND Health Experiment.* Cambridge, MA: Harvard University Press.

Newhouse, J. P., W. G. Manning, C. N. Morris, et al. (1981) Some interim results from a controlled trial of cost sharing in health insurance. *N Engl J Med* 305 (25): 1501–1507.

Oberlander, J., T. Marmor, Jacobs, L. (2001). Rationing medical care: Rhetoric and reality in the Oregon Health Plan. *CMAJ* 164 (11): 1583–1587.

OECD. (2024) OECD Health Statistics 2024.

Patel, N, Singhal S. (2024) What to Expect in US Healthcare in 2024 and beyond. McKinsey and Company. Accessed at https://www.mckinsey.com/industries/healthcare/ our-insights/what-to-expect-in- us-healthca re-in-2024-and-beyond#/.

Porter, M. E. (2010). What is value in health care?*New England Journal of Medicine* 363 (26): 2477-2481.

Plested, W. G. (2006) Here we go again: Same SGR song, newest version. *AM News.* October 16. http://www.ama-assn.org/amednews/2006/10/116/edc a1016.htm. Accessed October 31, 2007.

Rao, N. (2024) 2024 Healthcare Services Outlook: Challenges and Opportunities. McKinsey and Company. Accessed at https://www.mckinsey.com/industries/healthcare/our-insights/2024-healthcare-services-outlook- challenges-and-opportunities.

Rosenthal, M. B., and R. A. Dudley. (2007) Pay-for-performance: Will the latest payment trend improve care? *JAMA.* 297 (7): 740–744.

Rosenthal, M. B., B. E. Landon, S. T. Normand, R. G. Frank, T. S. Ahmad, and A. M. Epstein. (2007) Employers' use of value-based purchasing strategies. *JAMA* 298 (19): 2281–2288.

Saltman, R. B., Ferroussier-Davis, O. (2000) The concept of stewardship in health policy. *Bulletin of the World Health Organization* 78 (6): 732-739.

Siu, A.L., F. A. Sonnenberg, W. G. Manning, et al. (1986) Inappropriate use of hospitals in a randomized trial of health insurance plans. *N Engl J Med* 315 (20): 1259–1266.

Starr, P. (1982) *The social transformation of American medicine.* New York, New York: Basic Books, Inc.

Steinbrook, R. (2015) The Repeal of Medicare's Sustainable Growth Rate for Physician Payment. *JAMA* 313 (20): 2025–2026.

Turner, H. C., Archer, R. A., Downey, et al. (2021) An introduction to the main types of economic evaluations used for informing priority setting and resource allocation in healthcare: key features, uses, and limitations. *Frontiers in Public Health* 9: 722927.

Wells, D. A., J. S. Ross, A. S. Detsky. (2007) What is different about the market for health care? *JAMA* 2007; 298 (23): 2785–2787.

Woolhandler, S., D. U. Himmelstein. (2007) Consumer-directed healthcare: Except for the healthy and wealthy it's unwise. *J Gen Intern Med* 22 (6): 879–881.

CHAPTER 8

ESG FRAMEWORK FOR A SUSTAINABLE HEALTHCARE MARKETPLACE

8.1 BUSINESS DEVELOPMENT IN HEALTHCARE

The medical-industrial complex is undergoing significant transformations driven by technological advancements, evolving patient expectations, and shifting regulatory landscapes.

One of the most prominent developments is the integration of digital health technologies (Awad, 2021). Telemedicine, wearable devices, and mobile health apps are revolutionizing patient care by providing remote monitoring, real-time data sharing, and personalized treatment plans. These innovations enhance patient engagement, reduce healthcare costs, and improve access to care, particularly in underserved areas.

Another critical development is the rise of value-based care models, which shift the focus from volume to value. Instead of being compensated based on the number of services provided, healthcare providers are rewarded for improving patient outcomes and reducing costs (Lewis, 2022). This approach encourages preventive care, chronic disease management, and coordinated care, leading to better health outcomes and more efficient use of resources. It also necessitates closer collaboration between healthcare providers, payers, and patients, fostering a more integrated healthcare system.

Artificial Intelligence (AI) and data analytics are also playing transformative roles in healthcare (Secinaro et al., 2021; Kahn et al., 2020). AI-powered tools assist in diagnostics, treatment recommendations, and predictive analytics, enabling more accurate and timely interventions. For instance, machine learning algorithms can analyze medical images with high precision, aiding in early detection of diseases such as cancer. Big data analytics helps identify trends and patterns in patient populations, informing public health strategies and personalized medicine initiatives. These technologies not only enhance clinical decision-making but also streamline administrative processes, reducing the burden on healthcare professionals.

Personalized medicine is another burgeoning area, driven by advances in genomics and biotechnology (Hassan et al., 2022). By tailoring treatments to individual genetic profiles along with epigenetic expression, healthcare providers can offer more effective and targeted therapies, minimizing adverse effects and improving patient outcomes. This approach is particularly impactful in the treatment of complex diseases such as cancer, where personalized therapies can significantly increase survival rates. The growth of biopharmaceuticals and precision medicine is also fostering partnerships between healthcare providers, research institutions, and biotech companies, accelerating the development of innovative treatments.

Lastly, the emphasis on people-centered care is reshaping the healthcare landscape (Huffstetler et al., 2023). Patients today expect more than just medical treatment; they seek holistic and integrated care experiences that consider their physical, emotional, and social well-being. Healthcare providers are responding by enhancing patient communication, improving medical care environments, and offering supportive services such as mental health counseling and wellness programs. This shift towards a more holistic, integrated, and comprehensive approach not only improves the patient experience, patient satisfaction and health outcomes but also strengthens the overall healthcare delivery system by addressing the broader determinants of health; social, economic, environmental, and commercial.

These contemporary developments are collectively driving a more efficient, effective, and people-centered healthcare system. By embracing digital health technologies, value-based care models, AI and data analytics, personalized medicine, and holistic patient care, the healthcare industry is poised to meet the evolving needs of patients while achieving sustainable growth and innovation towards successful transformation to the Quintuple Aim (Nundy et al., 2022); a positive patient and provider experience, positive health outcomes for both individuals and populations, and closing of health disparities in demand of health equity.

8.2 ENVIRONMENTAL FOOTPRINT OF THE HEALTHCARE INDUSTRY

The healthcare industry, while committed to improving health outcomes, has a substantial environmental footprint primarily resulting from its operational activities (Chung and Meltzer, 2009; Lenzen et al., 2020). Hospitals and healthcare facilities are significant consumers of energy, water, and materials, and they generate a considerable amount of waste. The energy consumption in healthcare facilities is particularly high due to the need for continuous operation of medical equipment, HVAC systems, lighting, and other essential services. Hospitals, which operate 24/7, often require intensive energy use to maintain critical environments such as operating rooms and intensive care units. This high-energy demand contributes significantly to high volumes of greenhouse gas emissions, with healthcare facilities ranking among the highest energy consumers in the commercial sector.

A critical aspect of the healthcare industry's environmental footprint is its water usage. Healthcare facilities use vast quantities of water for various purposes, including sanitation, sterilization, and patient care. The reliance on water-intensive processes, such as laundering hospital linens, and operating cooling systems, adds to a hospital's overall environmental impact. Managing water usage efficiently and implementing water-saving technologies are essential steps to mitigate this impact (Peters et al., 2018). However, the challenge lies in balancing the need for rigorous hygiene and sanitation standards with the imperative to conserve water resources.

Waste generation in the healthcare sector is substantial and complex, comprising various types of waste, including general waste, hazardous waste, and medical waste. Medical waste, which includes items like used needles, contaminated dressings, and pharmaceutical products, poses significant disposal challenges due to its potential to spread infections and harmful substances. The proper handling and disposal of medical waste are critical to minimize environmental contamination and public health risks. Additionally, the widespread use of single-use medical supplies and packaging contributes to the high volume of waste generated, further exacerbating the environmental burden (Windfield et al., 2015).

The healthcare industry also has a significant impact through its supply chain operations (Jacobs, 2018). The production, transportation, and disposal of medical supplies and pharmaceuticals involve considerable resource use and emissions. The procurement of medical equipment, pharmaceuticals, and other supplies often involves complex global supply chains, which contribute to carbon emissions and environmental degradation. By adopting sustainable procurement practices, such as sourcing from environmentally responsible suppliers and reducing the reliance on single-use items, healthcare organizations can mitigate the environmental impact of their supply chains.

Efforts to reduce the environmental footprint of healthcare operations are gaining momentum. Many healthcare facilities are adopting green building standards, such as LEED certification, to improve energy and water efficiency, reduce waste, and create healthier indoor environments (Sentman, 2009). Implementing energy-efficient technologies, such as LED lighting, energy management systems, and renewable energy sources, can significantly lower energy consumption and emissions.

Waste reduction initiatives, such as recycling programs, reprocessing of medical devices, and the use of biodegradable materials, are also being explored to address the waste challenge. Water conservation measures, including the use of low-flow fixtures and water-efficient landscaping, help reduce water usage without compromising hygiene standards.

The environmental footprint of the healthcare industry's operations is substantial, driven by high energy and water consumption, significant waste generation, and complex supply chains. Addressing these environmental impacts requires a comprehensive approach that integrates sustainable practices into all aspects of healthcare operations (Lenzen et al., 2020). By adopting energy-efficient technologies, improving water management, reducing waste, and promoting sustainable procurement, healthcare organizations can significantly reduce their environmental footprint while continuing to provide high-quality care.

Eckelman et al (2020) summarize the importance of holding US healthcare entities accountable for human disease as a public health imperative:

> "...US health care activities contribute to substantial quantities of environmental emissions and disease burden, contrary to the mission to "First, do no harm." Health care organizations should take concrete steps to measure and reduce their carbon pollution. Mandated emissions reporting would inform science-based interventions and facilitate rapid adoption of sustainable health care practices that could dramatically reduce health care pollution and improve public health."

8.3 ESG MEASURES IN HEALTHCARE SYSTEMS

Environmental, Social, and Governance (ESG) measures in healthcare delivery are critical for ensuring that healthcare systems operate effectively, sustainably, equitably, and ethically. These measures address the diverse impacts of healthcare organizations on the environment, society, and internal governance, fostering a comprehensive approach to healthcare that benefits all stakeholders. (Lueng et al., 2023; Chime, 2024; Filipiak et al., 2021)

8.3.1 ENVIRONMENTAL MEASURES

Environmental measures in healthcare delivery focus on reducing the ecological footprint of healthcare facilities and operations. Key initiatives include:

1. Energy Efficiency and Renewable Energy. Healthcare facilities can invest in energy-efficient technologies and renewable energy sources to reduce their carbon emissions. This includes upgrading to LED lighting, using energy-efficient HVAC systems, and installing solar panels or wind turbines.

2. Waste Management. Effective waste management practices are essential in healthcare to minimize environmental impact. This involves reducing, reusing, and recycling materials where possible, as well as proper disposal of hazardous medical waste. Implementing single-use plastics reduction programs and promoting the use of sustainable materials also contribute to waste management efforts.

3. Sustainable Procurement. Adopting sustainable procurement practices throughout the medical supply chain ensures that the products and services used by healthcare facilities are environmentally friendly. This includes purchasing from suppliers who prioritize sustainability, opting for products with minimal packaging, and choosing reusable or recyclable medical supplies.

4. Water Conservation. Healthcare facilities can implement water-saving technologies and practices to reduce water consumption. This can involve installing low-flow fixtures, using water-efficient landscaping, and recycling water where appropriate.

8.3.2 SOCIAL MEASURES

Social measures in healthcare delivery focus on promoting cultural humility, empathy, equity, inclusivity, and community well-being. Key initiatives include:

1. Health Equity. Ensuring equitable access to healthcare services for all populations, particularly marginalized and underserved communities. This involves addressing social determinants of health, such as safe housing, education, and income, and developing targeted programs to reduce health disparities.

2. Community Engagement. Building strong relationships with the community through outreach programs, partnerships with local organizations, and active involvement in community health initiatives. This engagement helps healthcare providers understand and address the specific health needs of the community.

3. Employee Wellness and Well-being. Promoting the wellness and well-being of healthcare workers by providing a safe and supportive work environment, offering professional development opportunities, and ensuring fair labor practices. Supporting mental health and work-life balance for employees is also foundational to recruitment and retention of a strong and professional healthcare workforce.

4. People-Centered Care. Ensuring that healthcare delivery is people-centered, with a focus on improving the people experience and health outcomes. This involves providing culturally competent care, involving patients in shared decision-making, and offering education and support for self-management of health conditions.

8.3.3 GOVERNANCE MEASURES

Governance measures in healthcare delivery focus on ensuring transparency, accountability, and ethical conduct within healthcare organizations. Key initiatives include:

1. Ethical Leadership. Establishing strong leadership that prioritizes ethical decision-making and truthfulness. This involves setting clear ethical standards and evidence-based health management ensuring that healthcare leaders at all levels adhere to these principles and practices.

2. Transparency and Accountability. Implementing transparent reporting practices and holding healthcare organizations accountable for their actions. This includes regular disclosure of financial performance, environmental impact, and social initiatives, as well as engaging with stakeholders to gather voice of the customer and address concerns.

3. Compliance and Risk Management. Ensuring compliance with all relevant laws and regulations, and implementing robust risk management practices to identify, assess, and mitigate potential risks. This includes maintaining patient privacy and data security, adhering to clinical and safety standards, and addressing any unethical behavior promptly.

4. Diversity and Inclusion. Promoting diversity and inclusion within the healthcare workforce and leadership. This involves implementing policies and practices that foster an inclusive environment, supporting the recruitment and retention of diverse talent, and addressing any barriers to equal opportunity.

Integrating ESG measures into healthcare delivery ensures that healthcare organizations operate responsibly and sustainably, resulting in better health outcomes, stronger communities, and a healthier planet. By considering environmental, social, and governance factors, healthcare providers can develop a more resilient and equitable healthcare system that addresses the needs of both current and future generations.

8.4 BASICS OF ESG REPORTING FOR THE AMERICAN HEALTHCARE DELIVERY SYSTEM

ESG reporting is a critical tool for a US healthcare delivery system committed to sustainability, transparency, and accountability. At its core, ESG reporting involves the systematic disclosure of information related to any healthcare entity's (e.g., hospital, health system, medical supply chain) environmental, social, and governance practices. This process provides stakeholders—including investors, customers, employees, and regulators—with a clear understanding of the company's efforts to manage ESG-related risks and opportunities. Effective ESG reporting begins with identifying the key ESG issues relevant to the business and its stakeholders. This materiality assessment helps organizations prioritize the most significant impacts and opportunities, ensuring that the report focuses on areas that matter most to their audience (Gabius, 2023; Arvidsson et al., 2022; Sellhorn et al., 2024).

Environmental reporting involves the disclosure of data related to a company's environmental impact, including carbon footprint, energy consumption, water usage, waste management, and efforts to mitigate climate change. Companies should report on their strategies to reduce greenhouse gas emissions, enhance energy efficiency, and promote sustainable resource use. Key performance indicators might include total carbon emissions, percentage of energy from renewable sources, water consumption per unit of production, and waste recycling rates. These indicators provide a quantifiable measure of environmental performance and progress over time, demonstrating the company's commitment to sustainability.

Social reporting covers a broad range of topics related to a company's impact on people and society. This includes labor practices, employee well-being, diversity and inclusion, community engagement, collective impact, social justice, and human rights. Companies should provide information on their workforce demographics, employee training and development programs, health and safety initiatives, and efforts to promote a diverse and inclusive workplace. Additionally, reporting on community involvement and philanthropic activities highlights the company's contribution to social well-being. Key performance indicators such as employee retention rates, OSHA-recordable workplace injury rates, diversity ratios, and community investment levels offer insight into the company's social performance and its commitment to positive societal impact.

Governance reporting focuses on the systems and processes that ensure the company is managed ethically and transparently. This includes information on board composition and diversity, executive compensation, shareholder rights and responsibilities, and risk management practices. Companies should disclose their governance structures, including the roles and responsibilities of the board of directors and executive management, and any policies related to ethical conduct, anti-corruption, and compliance. Key performance indicators in governance reporting might include board diversity statistics, executive pay ratios, frequency of board meetings, ESG sub-committee reporting, and outcomes of shareholder votes. Robust governance reporting demonstrates a company's commitment to accountability and ethical management.

The process of ESG reporting for the US healthcare delivery system is no different than any other industry and involves not only the collection and analysis of relevant data but also the communication of this information in a clear, accessible, and transparent manner. The medical-industrial complex and its constituent organizations typically publish their ESG reports annually, often as part of their broader sustainability or corporate responsibility reports. These reports should be guided by recognized reporting frameworks and standards, such as the Global Reporting Initiative (GRI) (Rimmel, 2020), the Sustainability Accounting Standards Board (SASB) (Schooley et al, 2015), and the Task Force on Climate-related Financial Disclosures (TCFD) (Eccles et al., 2019). Adhering to these frameworks ensures that the reports are comprehensive, comparable, and credible, enhancing trust and confidence among stakeholders.

Finally, ESG reporting is not just about compliance but about continuous improvement and stakeholder engagement (Sampson, 2023). Companies should use the insights gained from ESG reporting to inform their sustainability strategies and drive performance improvements. Regularly updating stakeholders on progress, challenges, and future goals fosters transparency and accountability. Engaging with stakeholders through surveys, consultations, and feedback mechanisms can provide valuable insights into their expectations and concerns, helping to align the company's ESG efforts with stakeholder priorities. By embedding ESG reporting into their business strategy, companies can enhance their sustainability performance, build stronger relationships with stakeholders, and create long-term value.

8.5 FOUNDATIONAL ELEMENTS FOR APPLYING ESG IN SUSTAINABLE HEALTHCARE SYSTEM STRATEGIES

The successful application of Environmental, Social, and Governance (ESG) principles in sustainable healthcare strategies relies on a few foundational elements (Dathe et al., 2024; Leung et al., 2023).

One of the primary elements is a robust commitment to environmental sustainability. This involves adopting green principles and practices such as reducing energy consumption, managing waste effectively, and minimizing carbon emissions. Healthcare organizations can implement energy-efficient technologies, invest in renewable energy sources, and adopt sustainable building practices for new facilities. Additionally, reducing the use of harmful chemicals and promoting the use of recyclable materials in medical supplies can significantly lower the environmental footprint. These practices not only contribute to global sustainability efforts but also help in reducing operational costs and enhancing the organization's reputation among environmentally conscious stakeholders.

Another critical foundational element is fostering social responsibility within the medical-industrial complex. This includes addressing all determinants of health (i.e., social, economic, environmental, and commercial), such as economic stability, education, food instability, toxic exposures, and access to healthcare services. Healthcare organizations should aim to provide equitable care to all populations, especially underserved and marginalized communities, with cultural humility and empathy. Enhancing workforce diversity and inclusion is also essential, as a diverse workforce can better meet the needs of diverse patient populations. Additionally, prioritizing employee wellness and well-being and ensuring fair labor practices contribute to a positive organizational culture and improved people care. By addressing these social aspects, healthcare organizations can build stronger, healthier communities and foster greater trust, transparency, accountability, and loyalty among patients and employees.

Strong governance structures are equally vital in embedding ESG principles into healthcare strategies. This involves establishing clear policies and procedures to ensure ethical conduct, compliance with regulations, and transparency and accountability in decision-making processes. Healthcare organizations should develop comprehensive governance frameworks that include regular audits, risk-management assessments, and stakeholder engagement mechanisms. Engaging stakeholders such as patients, employees, investors, and community members in decision-making processes ensures that the organization's strategies align with the preferences, needs, values, and expectations of its stakeholders. Effective governance also involves continuous monitoring and reporting of ESG performance, allowing organizations to measure progress, identify areas for improvement, and maintain accountability.

Integrating ESG principles into healthcare strategies also requires a commitment to continuous innovation and improvement. This means staying abreast of technological advancements and adopting new tools and practices that support sustainability goals. For instance, leveraging digital health technologies can reduce the need for physical infrastructure and travel, thereby lowering carbon emissions. Additionally, investing in research and development of sustainable medical practices and products can drive innovation and set new standards in the industry. Continuous education and training for healthcare professionals on ESG issues and sustainable principles and practices are also crucial, ensuring that the workforce is equipped to support and drive the organization's sustainability initiatives.

In summary, the foundational elements of applying ESG principles in sustainable healthcare strategies include a strong commitment to environmental sustainability, fostering social responsibility, establishing robust governance structures, and a dedication to continuous innovation and improvement. By focusing on these elements, healthcare organizations can create value not only for themselves but also for their patients, employees, and the broader community. This holistic and integrative approach ensures that sustainability is embedded in the healthcare organization's core operations, leading to long-term success and resilience.

8.6 MATERIALIZING ESG IN THE SUSTAINABLE BUSINESS OF HEALTHCARE

Materializing ESG (Environmental, Social, and Governance) principles in the healthcare sector requires a strategic integration of these principles into core business operations and long-term planning (Chui et al., 2023; Rane et al., 2024; Leung et al., 2023).

For environmental sustainability, healthcare organizations can implement energy-efficient technologies, reduce medical waste, and minimize their carbon footprint. This can be achieved by adopting renewable energy sources, optimizing water usage, and implementing green building standards for new facilities (Sentman, 2009; Vierra, 2016). For example, hospitals can invest in solar panels, energy-efficient lighting, and HVAC systems to reduce energy consumption. Additionally, reducing single-use plastics and properly managing medical waste can significantly decrease environmental impact. These practices not only contribute to global sustainability goals but also lead to cost savings and enhanced organizational reputation.

Social responsibility in healthcare involves addressing social determinants of health, promoting equity, and improving community health outcomes. Healthcare organizations can work towards ensuring that all patients, regardless of socioeconomic status, have access to high-quality care. This can be done by expanding telehealth services, creating outreach programs for underserved populations, and partnering with community organizations to address social needs such as housing, nutrition, and education. Furthermore, fostering a diverse and inclusive workforce is essential. Healthcare providers can implement policies and practices that promote diversity and inclusion in hiring, provide cultural competency training, and support the career development and advancement of underrepresented groups. These efforts not only improve patient care but also enhance employee recruitment and retention and organizational culture.

Strong governance practices are crucial for embedding ESG principles into the business model of healthcare organizations. This includes establishing transparent decision-making processes, robust risk management frameworks, and ethical business practices. Effective governance requires regular audits, compliance with regulations, and transparent reporting on ESG performance. By creating a governance structure that includes ESG goals, healthcare organizations can ensure accountability and align their operations with stakeholder expectations. Engaging stakeholders such as patients, employees, investors, and community members in governance processes ensures that diverse perspectives are considered and that the organization's strategies are responsive to the needs and expectations of those they serve.

To effectively materialize ESG principles, healthcare organizations need to integrate them into their strategic planning and operational workflows. This involves setting clear ESG objectives, aligning them with business goals, and developing actionable plans to achieve them. For instance, organizations can set targets for reducing greenhouse gas emissions, improving patient satisfaction scores, and increasing workforce diversity. These targets should be accompanied by detailed action plans, timelines, and assigned responsibilities. Regular monitoring and reporting on performance and progress towards these targets are essential to ensure accountability and continuous improvement. By embedding ESG into strategic planning, healthcare organizations can drive sustainable growth and resilience.

Innovation and technology play a significant role in materializing ESG in healthcare. Leveraging digital health technologies, such as telemedicine, electronic health records (EHRs), and AI-powered diagnostics, can enhance efficiency, reduce environmental impact, and improve health outcomes. For example, telemedicine reduces the need for physical visits, lowering the carbon footprint associated with patient travel. AI and data analytics can optimize resource use, predict patient needs, and personalize medical care, leading to better health outcomes and more efficient use of resources. Investing in research and development of sustainable medical practices and products also supports the advancement of ESG goals. By embracing innovation, healthcare organizations can achieve sustainable business growth while adhering to ESG principles.

In summary, materializing ESG in the sustainable business of healthcare involves integrating environmental sustainability, social responsibility, and strong governance into core operations and strategic planning. This requires adopting green building practices, addressing all determinants of health, promoting equality and equity, and establishing robust governance frameworks. By setting clear ESG objectives, leveraging innovation, and engaging stakeholders, healthcare organizations can create sustainable value for patients, employees, communities, and investors, ensuring long-term success and resilience.

8.7 A ROADMAP FOR IMPLEMENTING ESG PRACTICES IN THE MEDICAL-INDUSTRIAL COMPLEX

Implementing ESG practices throughout the medical-industrial complex requires a comprehensive and structured roadmap that outlines clear steps and objectives (Haar, 2024). The first step in this roadmap is to conduct a thorough materiality assessment of the current state of ESG practices within the organization. This involves evaluating existing policies, practices, procedures, and performance in environmental sustainability, social responsibility, and governance. Gathering data on energy usage, waste management, workforce diversity, patient satisfaction, and compliance with regulatory standards provides a baseline from which to measure progress. Engaging stakeholders, including employees, patients, investors, and community members, in this materiality assessment process ensures a holistic, integrated, and comprehensive understanding of the healthcare organization's strengths, weaknesses, opportunities and threats (Filipiak et al., 2021)

The next step is to develop a strategic plan that aligns ESG objectives with the healthcare organization's overall mission, vision, and strategic goals (Sepetis et al., 2024). This plan should include specific, measurable, achievable, relevant, and time-bound (SMART) goals for each of the ESG dimensions. For environmental sustainability, goals might include reducing carbon emissions, increasing energy efficiency, and minimizing medical waste. Social responsibility goals could focus on improving access and navigation to clinical care, enhancing workforce diversity and inclusion, and supporting community-based organizations and their community health initiatives. Governance goals might include strengthening compliance frameworks, increasing transparency, and improving stakeholder engagement. The strategic plan should also outline the resources required, including financial investments, technology, and personnel, to achieve these goals.

Once the strategic plan is in place, the next phase involves implementing targeted initiatives to achieve the outlined goals. For environmental sustainability, this could involve investing in energy-efficient technologies, implementing medical waste reduction programs, and adopting green building practices. Social initiatives might include expanding telehealth services to improve access to care, creating programs to support workforce diversity and inclusion, and partnering with community organizations to address all determinants of health.

Governance initiatives could focus on enhancing compliance training for staff, establishing robust risk management frameworks, and improving transparency through regular ESG reporting. Each initiative should have a clear implementation timeline, assigned responsibilities, and key performance indicators for tracking progress.

Monitoring and evaluation are critical components of the roadmap, ensuring that the healthcare organization stays on track to meet its ESG goals. Establishing a robust monitoring system involves regularly collecting and analyzing data on key performance indicators related to environmental, social, and governance policies and practices. This data should be used to generate regular actionable reports, real-time dashboards, and annual scorecards with benchmarks that provide insights into progress, identify areas for improvement, and inform decision-making. Additionally, engaging stakeholders in the evaluation process helps maintain accountability and ensures that the organization's ESG efforts align with their expectations, preferences, needs and values.

The final step in the roadmap is continuous improvement and adaptation. ESG practices and standards are continually evolving, (e.g., annual changes to the global reporting initiative), and healthcare organizations must remain agile to anticipate and respond to these new challenges and opportunities in real time. This involves regularly reviewing and updating the strategic plan, incorporating feedback from stakeholders, and staying informed about emerging trends and best practices in ESG. Continuous education and development for staff on ESG issues are also essential, ensuring that the workforce remains knowledgeable and committed to the healthcare organization's sustainability goals. By cultivating a culture of continuous quality improvement, healthcare organizations can maintain the effectiveness, relevance, and impact of their ESG practices over the long term.

A structured roadmap for implementing ESG practices in healthcare organizations involves assessing the current state, developing a strategic plan with SMART goals, implementing targeted initiatives, monitoring and evaluating progress, and continuously improving and adapting strategies. By following this roadmap, healthcare organizations can effectively integrate ESG principles into their daily operations, creating sustainable value for their patients, employees, communities, and stakeholders.

8.8 VALUE CREATION FOR ESG IN THE HEALTHCARE INDUSTRY

The importance of Environmental, Social, and Governance (ESG) principles is growing in the healthcare industry. ESG initiatives can lead to significant value creation by promoting sustainability, enhancing social responsibility, and ensuring strong governance (Sherman et al, 2020). These principles not only align with the ethical imperatives of healthcare organizations but also drive financial performance, operational efficiency, and a positive patient experience.

From an environmental perspective, healthcare organizations that adopt sustainable practices can reduce their carbon footprint and minimize medical waste, contributing to global efforts to combat climate change. Implementing energy-efficient systems, reducing single-use plastics, and promoting telehealth can lower operational costs and improve resource allocation. Additionally, environmentally conscious policies and practices can enhance a healthcare organization's reputation, attracting patients and investors who prioritize sustainability.

Social factors are equally crucial in value creation. Healthcare organizations committed to social responsibility can improve community health outcomes by addressing all determinants of health. Fostering a diverse and inclusive workforce enhances innovation and patient care, as a variety of perspectives and experiences lead to better hard and soft skill development, critical thinking, problem solving, and decision-making. Furthermore, ensuring patient safety, privacy, and satisfaction builds trust, truthfulness, and loyalty, which are essential for long-term success.

Governance plays a pivotal role in maintaining the integrity and accountability of healthcare organizations. Strong governance frameworks ensure compliance with regulations, ethical conduct, and transparent decision-making. By prioritizing governance, healthcare organizations can mitigate risks, prevent fraud, and attract investment. Effective governance also involves stakeholder engagement, which includes patients, employees, investors, and the community, ensuring that the organization's strategies align with the preferences, needs, and value expectations of its stakeholders.

The integration of ESG principles and practices within the medical-industrial complex not only addresses environmental and social challenges but also enhances organizational performance and resilience. By committing to sustainable policies and practices, social responsibility, and robust governance, healthcare organizations can create substantial value, benefiting both society and their triple-bottom line reporting of ESG (Crace et al., 2023; Chui et al., 2023; Leung et al., 2023.).

8.9 REFERENCES

Arvidsson, S., Dumay, J. (2022). Corporate ESG reporting quantity, quality and performance: Where to now for environmental policy and practice?*Business Strategy and the Environment*31 (3): 1091-1110.

Awad, A., Trenfield, S. J., Pollard, T. D., et al. (2021) Connected healthcare: Improving patient care using digital health technologies.*Advanced Drug Delivery Reviews*178: 113958.

Chime, C. (2024) ESG Risks and Integration by Healthcare Companies.

Chiu, W. K., Fong, B. Y. F. (2023) Environmental, social and governance and sustainable development in healthcare.*Recent Trends of Research and Education in ESG and Sustainability*, 99-112.

Crace, L., Gehman, J. (2023) What really explains ESG performance? Disentangling the asymmetrical drivers of the triple bottom line. *Organization& Environment* 36 (1): 150-178.

Chung, JW, Meltzer, DO. (2009) Estimate of the Carbon Footprint of the US Health Care Sector. JAMA 302 (18):1970–1972.

Dathe, T., Helmold, M., Dathe, R., et al. (2024) *Implementing Environmental, Social and Governance (ESG) Principles for Sustainable Businesses: A Practical Guide in Sustainability Management.* Springer Nature.

Eccles, R. G., Krzus, M. P. (2019) Implementing the task force on climate-related financial disclosures recommendations: An assessment of corporate readiness. *Schmalenbach Business Review* 71: 287-293.

Eckelman, M. J., Huang, K., Lagasse, R., et.al. (2020). Health Care Pollution and Public Health Damage in The United States: An Update. *Health affairs (Project Hope)*, *39* (12), 2071–2079.

Filipiak, B. Z., Kiestrzyn, M. (2021) Potential ESG Risks in Entities of the Healthcare System. *In* Adapting and Mitigating Environmental, Social, and Governance Risk in Business (pp. 74-102). IGI Global.

Gabius, K. (2023) 8.1 Basics of Sustainability. *Sustainable Business Management* 129.

Haar, G. (2024). Developing a Sustainability Roadmap. In: The Great Transition to a Green and Circular Economy. Springer, Cham.

Hassan, M., Awan, F. M., Naz, A., et al. (2022) Innovations in genomics and big data analytics for personalized medicine and health care: A review. *International Journal of Molecular Sciences* 23 (9): 4645.

Huffstetler, A. N., Phillips Jr, R. L., Leyns, et al. (2023). People-centered health services. *In*Person Centered Medicine(pp. 135-150). Cham: Springer International Publishing.

Jacobs, F. R., Chase, R. B. (2018).*Operations and supply chain management*. McGraw-Hill.

Khan, Z. F., Alotaibi, S. R. (2020) Applications of artificial intelligence and big data analytics in m-health: A healthcare system perspective.*Journal of Healthcare Engineering*1: 8894694.

Lenzen, M., Malik, A., Li, M., et al. (2020) The environmental footprint of health care: a global assessment.*The Lancet Planetary Health* 4 (7): e271-e279.

Lewis, S. (2022) Value-based healthcare: is it the way forward? *Future Healthcare Journal*9 (3): 211-215.

Leung, T. C. H., You, C. S. X. (2023). ESG Application in Sustainable Development of the Healthcare Industry. *In*Environmental, Social and Governance and Sustainable Development in Healthcare(pp. 47-64). Singapore: Springer Nature Singapore.

Nundy, S., Cooper, L. A., Mate, K. S. (2022) The quintuple aim for health care improvement: a new imperative to advance health equity.*JAMA*327 (6): 521-522.

Peters, A., Otter, J., Moldovan, A., et al. (2018) Keeping hospitals clean and safe without breaking the bank; Summary of the Healthcare Cleaning Forum 2018.

Rane, N., Choudhary, S., Rane, J. (2024). Artificial intelligence driven approaches to strengthening Environmental, Social, and Governance (ESG) criteria in sustainable business practices: a review.*Social, and Governance (ESG) Criteria in Sustainable Business Practices: A review*.

Rimmel, G. (2020) Global reporting initiative. *In*Accounting for Sustainability(pp. 111-125). Routledge.

Sampson, C. J. (2023) Unlocking ESG in Healthcare: Governance Holds the Key.*Frontiers of Health Services Management*39 (3): 1-4.

Schooley, D. K., English, D. M. (2015) SASB: A pathway to sustainability reporting in the United States.*The CPA Journal*85 (4): 22.

Secinaro, S., Calandra, D., Secinaro, A., et al. (2021) The role of artificial intelligence in healthcare: a structured literature review.*BMC Medical Informatics and Decision Making*21: 1-23.

Sellhorn, T., Wagner, V. (2024) The forces that shape mandatory ESG reporting. *In*Research Handbook on Environmental, Social and Corporate Governance(pp. 269-292). Edward Elgar Publishing.

Sentman, S. D. (2009). Healthy buildings: Green building standards, benefits, and incentives.*The Journal of Biolaw and Business*12 (1): 4.

Sepetis, A., Rizos, F., Pierrakos, et al. (2024) A sustainable model for healthcare systems: The innovative approach of ESG and digital transformation. *Healthcare* 12 (2): 156.

Sherman JD, Thiel C, MacNeill A, et al. (2020) The green print: advancement of environmental sustainability in health care. Resour Conserv Recycling. 161:104882.

Windfield, E. S., Brooks, M. S. L. (2015) Medical waste management–A review.*Journal of Environmental Management*163: 98-108.

Vierra, S. (2016) Green building standards and certification systems. *National Institute of Building Sciences,* Washington, DC.

CHAPTER 9

THE ANTHROPOCENE AND HEALTHCARE STEWARDSHIP

9.1 ANTHROPOCENE CLIMATE CHANGE AND HEALTHCARE STEWARDSHIP

Anthropocene (i.e., man-made) climate change significantly impacts healthcare stewardship by exacerbating the frequency and severity of health crises, thereby straining healthcare resources and infrastructure (Barna et al., 2020, Shaw et al., 2021; Roka, 2020).

As climate change leads to more extreme weather events such as heatwaves, floods, and hurricanes, the incidence of climate-related health issues rises, including heat-related illnesses, respiratory problems from increased air pollution, and injuries from natural disasters (Tong et al., 2022). Healthcare systems must allocate additional resources to address these emergencies, often at the expense of other areas of clinical care. This increased demand challenges healthcare stewardship efforts to efficiently manage resources while maintaining high-quality care and preparedness for ongoing and future climate-related events.

Additionally, climate change influences the spread of infectious diseases, complicating healthcare stewardship (Morand et al. 2020). Warmer temperatures and changing precipitation patterns can expand the habitats of disease vectors like mosquitoes and ticks, leading to the spread of diseases such as malaria, dengue fever, and Lyme disease into previously unaffected regions. Healthcare systems must adapt by investing in surveillance, prevention, and treatment programs for these emerging infectious disease threats. This necessitates careful planning and resource allocation to prevent and manage outbreaks, emphasizing the importance of proactive and adaptable healthcare stewardship in a changing climate.

Climate change also exacerbates existing health disparities, making healthcare stewardship even more challenging (Sasser et al., 2018). Vulnerable populations, including the elderly, low-income communities, and those with preexisting health conditions, are disproportionately affected by climate-related health issues. These groups often have less access to healthcare and fewer resources to cope with climate impacts. Healthcare stewardship must prioritize equity by ensuring that resources are distributed fairly and that all populations have access to necessary care and support. This requires targeted interventions and healthy public policies aimed at reducing health disparities and improving resilience among the most vulnerable.

The environmental impacts of climate change necessitate a shift towards sustainable healthcare practices as part of responsible stewardship. Healthcare facilities are significant contributors to greenhouse gas emissions and environmental pollution. To mitigate their environmental footprint, healthcare systems must adopt sustainable practices such as reducing energy consumption, minimizing medical waste, and sourcing eco-friendly products. These efforts not only contribute to global climate mitigation goals but also align with the principles of healthcare stewardship by promoting long-term sustainability and essential public health services integration (Buse et al., 2018). Investing in green infrastructure and practices can also result in cost savings, which can be redirected to patient care and other critical operating expenses.

Finally, climate change underscores the importance of integrating climate resilience into healthcare stewardship strategies (Folke et al., 2020;. This involves building healthcare infrastructure that can withstand extreme weather events, ensuring reliable supply chains for medical supplies, and developing emergency preparedness and response plans that address climate-related existential health threats. By incorporating climate resilience into healthcare planning, systems can better anticipate and respond to the challenges posed by a changing climate. This proactive approach is essential for maintaining the integrity and effectiveness of healthcare stewardship in the Anthropocene era, ensuring that healthcare systems remain robust and capable of delivering quality care amidst environmental uncertainties (Kareiva et al., 2016).

9.2 GREENHOUSE GAS EMISSIONS FROM THE HEALTHCARE INDUSTRY

Greenhouse gas (GHG) emissions from the healthcare industry can be categorized into three scopes, as defined by the Greenhouse Gas Protocol (Feist, 2018; Ghaemi et al., 2020)

Scope 1 emissions are direct emissions from sources owned or controlled by the healthcare organization. These include emissions from on-site combustion of fossil fuels in boilers, furnaces, and generators, as well as emissions from hospital-owned vehicles. For example, many hospitals operate on-site power plants or emergency backup generators that rely on diesel or natural gas, contributing significantly to Scope 1 emissions. Addressing these emissions requires transitioning to cleaner energy sources, enhancing energy efficiency, and adopting low-emission vehicle fleets.

Scope 2 emissions encompass indirect GHG emissions from the consumption of purchased electricity, steam, heating, and cooling. These emissions occur at the facilities where the energy is generated but are attributed to the healthcare organization that consumes the energy. Hospitals and healthcare facilities are typically large energy consumers due to their 24/7 operations and the need for high-powered medical equipment, extensive HVAC systems, and comprehensive lighting. To reduce Scope 2 emissions, healthcare organizations can invest in energy-efficient infrastructure, participate in demand response programs, and purchase renewable energy credits or directly source renewable energy through on-site installations like solar panels or off-site renewable energy agreements.

Scope 3 emissions are the most extensive and encompass all other indirect emissions that occur in the value chain of the reporting health organization. This includes emissions from activities such as the production and transportation of purchased goods and services, business travel, employee commuting, waste disposal, and the use of sold products. In the healthcare sector, Scope 3 emissions can be substantial due to the complex medical and non-medical supply chains involved in manufacturing medical equipment, pharmaceuticals, and other healthcare products. Furthermore, the logistics of delivering supplies, managing medical waste, and even the emissions associated with patient and employee travel contribute significantly to Scope 3 emissions. Reducing these emissions involves collaborating, cooperating, and coordinating with suppliers to promote sustainable practices, optimizing logistics to minimize transportation emissions, and encouraging alternative commuting options for employees, such as telecommuting or public transportation incentives.

Efforts to mitigate GHG emissions across all three scopes require a comprehensive and coordinated approach (Davis et al., 2000). For Scope 1 and 2 emissions, healthcare organizations can conduct energy audits to identify opportunities for efficiency improvements and retrofitting facilities with energy-efficient technologies. Implementing rigorous maintenance programs for heating and cooling systems and transitioning to low-carbon energy sources are also essential strategies. For Scope 3 emissions, engaging with suppliers to adopt greener practices, reducing the carbon footprint of procurement processes, and fostering a culture of sustainability within the organization are critical steps.

In conclusion, GHG emissions from the healthcare industry are significant and span across direct, indirect, and value chain-related activities, categorized into Scope 1, 2, and 3 emissions. By addressing these emissions through targeted strategies such as transitioning to renewable energy, enhancing energy efficiency, and promoting sustainable supply chain practices, healthcare organizations can substantially reduce their environmental impact. Integrating these efforts into a broader sustainability strategy not only helps mitigate climate change but also supports the medical-industrial complex's mission to protect and improve public health.

9.3 THE IMPORTANCE OF BIODIVERSITY AND CONSERVATION FOR HEALTHCARE STEWARDSHIP

Biodiversity and conservation play a critical role in healthcare stewardship by maintaining the balance of ecosystems, which directly impacts human health (WHO, 2021; Sharma et al., 2024).

Biodiversity refers to the variety of life on Earth, encompassing different species, genetic variations, and ecosystems. This diversity is essential for ecosystem resilience and the provision of ecosystem services, including clean air and water, fertile soil, and the regulation of climate. These services are foundational for human health, as they contribute to the availability of medicinal resources, nutritional security, and the prevention of diseases.

Medicinal resources derived from biodiversity are indispensable to modern healthcare (Khasim et al., 2020). Many pharmaceuticals are either directly extracted from plants, animals, and microorganisms or synthesized based on compounds found in nature. For instance, the rosy periwinkle has been instrumental in developing treatments for leukemia and Hodgkin's disease. Similarly, the diverse microbial life found in soil has given rise to numerous antibiotics. The loss of biodiversity threatens the discovery of new medicinal resources and the continued availability of existing ones, underscoring the need for conservation efforts to safeguard these biological treasures.

Conservation of biodiversity is also crucial for controlling disease vectors and maintaining ecological balances that prevent outbreaks (Lafferty, 2009). Healthy ecosystems regulate populations of disease-carrying organisms, such as mosquitoes, ticks, and rodents, thus reducing the incidence of diseases like malaria, Lyme disease, and hantavirus. Habitat destruction and climate change can disrupt these natural controls, leading to increased exposure to pathogens. By protecting and restoring natural habitats, conservation efforts help maintain these regulatory functions, thereby protecting human populations from emerging infectious diseases.

Furthermore, biodiversity contributes to nutritional security, which is a cornerstone of health (Iyiola et al., 2022). Diverse diets rich in various plant and animal species provide essential nutrients that are vital for human growth, development, and immune function. The erosion of genetic diversity in crops and livestock reduces the resilience of food systems to pests, diseases, and climate change, potentially leading to malnutrition and food insecurity. Conservation practices that promote agricultural biodiversity ensure the stability and sustainability of food supplies, supporting overall health and well-being.

The stewardship of biodiversity through conservation is vital for healthcare. It supports the discovery and development of medicines, controls disease vectors, maintains ecological balances, and ensures nutritional security. Protecting biodiversity is not only an environmental imperative but also a fundamental component of essential public health strategy and function.

9.4 AMERICAN HEALTHCARE DELIVERY SYSTEM'S ESG RESPONSE TO ANTHROPOCENE CLIMATE CHANGE

Environmental, Social, and Governance (ESG) criteria have become increasingly relevant in the context of Anthropocene climate change, particularly within U.S. healthcare delivery systems. Incorporating ESG principles into healthcare operations can enhance sustainability, social responsibility, and ethical governance, addressing the multifaceted challenges posed by climate change (Lueng et al, 2023; Nakielski, 2023).

From an environmental perspective, healthcare delivery systems can significantly reduce their carbon footprint by adopting green building standards, improving energy efficiency, and investing in renewable energy sources (Mostepaniuk et al., 2023). By minimizing medical waste through robust recycling programs and sustainable procurement practices, healthcare facilities can lessen their environmental impact, contributing to broader climate change mitigation efforts.

On the social front, ESG principles advocate for equity and inclusivity within healthcare systems, crucial for addressing the health disparities exacerbated by climate change (NASEM, 2019). Vulnerable populations, such as low-income communities, the elderly, and those with chronic health conditions, often bear the brunt of climate-related health impacts. Healthcare delivery systems can incorporate ESG frameworks to ensure equitable access to care and resources, developing targeted programs that enhance the resilience of these at-risk groups. By fostering community engagement and partnerships, healthcare organizations can better understand and address the unique needs of diverse populations, promoting social justice and health equity.

Governance is another critical component of ESG in response to climate change, emphasizing transparency, accountability, and ethical decision-making within healthcare delivery systems (Churet et al., 2014). Strong governance structures can ensure that sustainability initiatives are effectively implemented and that environmental and social goals are met. This involves setting clear targets for reducing emissions, monitoring progress, and publicly reporting on outcomes. Additionally, healthcare organizations must prioritize ethical considerations in their operations, such as ensuring workforce development, fair labor practices, protecting patient privacy, and maintaining high standards of clinical care. By adhering to robust governance principles, healthcare systems can build trust with stakeholders and enhance their overall resilience to climate-related challenges.

Furthermore, integrating ESG criteria into healthcare delivery systems can drive innovation and long-term financial performance (Sepetis et al., 2024). Sustainable practices often lead to cost savings, such as reduced energy expenditures and waste disposal costs, which can be reinvested into patient care and facility improvements. ESG-focused healthcare organizations may also attract investment from socially responsible investors who prioritize sustainability and ethical governance. This financial support can fund further advancements in medical technology, infrastructure, and services, ultimately enhancing the quality and accessibility of healthcare. By aligning financial goals with ESG principles, healthcare delivery systems can achieve a balance between profitability and social responsibility (Bhattacharya et al., 2023).

Incorporating ESG principles into U.S. healthcare delivery systems is essential for adapting to and mitigating the impacts of Anthropocene climate change. It requires a holistic, integrated, and comprehensive approach that considers environmental sustainability, social responsibility and equity, and strong leadership through governance. By embracing these principles, healthcare organizations can not only improve their operational efficiency and financial performance but also contribute to the broader societal effort to combat climate change. This proactive stance ensures that healthcare systems are not only resilient and adaptable but also leaders in the global movement toward an all-encompassing sustainable and equitable future.

9.5 INTEGRATION OF ESG PRINCIPLES INTO HEALTHCARE STEWARDSHIP

The integration of Environmental, Social, and Governance (ESG) principles into healthcare stewardship creates a synergistic relationship that enhances the sustainability, equity, and ethical management of healthcare resources.

Environmental stewardship in healthcare involves implementing practices that reduce the environmental footprint of healthcare facilities, such as improving energy efficiency, minimizing waste, and adopting green procurement strategies. By aligning these efforts with ESG principles, healthcare organizations can achieve significant environmental benefits while maintaining high standards of patient care. This not only supports the broader goal of mitigating climate change but also ensures that healthcare operations are sustainable in the long term, conserving resources for future generations.

Social aspects of ESG align closely with healthcare stewardship by emphasizing the importance of equitable access to healthcare services and addressing health disparities. Healthcare stewardship aims to optimize resource allocation to improve patient outcomes and ensure that all individuals, regardless of their socio-economic status, receive high-quality medical care with cultural humility and empathy. ESG principles reinforce this by promoting social responsibility, health equity, and community engagement. For example, healthcare organizations can develop outreach programs that target underserved communities, providing education, proactive care, and treatment for conditions exacerbated by climate change. By prioritizing social responsibility and health equity, healthcare systems can create more inclusive and resilient communities, thereby fulfilling their stewardship responsibilities.

Governance, the third pillar of ESG, plays a crucial role in ensuring transparency, accountability, integrity, and trust in healthcare stewardship. Effective governance frameworks are essential for the ethical management of healthcare resources, ensuring that decisions are made in the best interest of patients and communities from a top-down and bottom-up leadership and communication framework. ESG principles advocate for robust governance structures that include strong healthy public policies, regular audits, and stakeholder engagement. These practices help healthcare organizations to maintain integrity and trust, critical components of successful stewardship. Transparent reporting on environmental and social initiatives allows healthcare providers to demonstrate their commitment to sustainability and health equity, building credibility and fostering confidence with individuals, their families, and the communities in which they serve.

The relationship between ESG and healthcare stewardship also drives innovation and continuous improvement. By embracing ESG principles, healthcare organizations are encouraged to explore new technologies and practices that enhance sustainability and efficiency. For example, investing in telehealth and digital health solutions can reduce the need for physical infrastructure and decrease the environmental impact of patient travel. Additionally, adopting sustainable medical supply chain practices can ensure the availability of essential medical supplies while minimizing environmental harm. These innovations not only support environmental and social goals but also improve the overall quality and accessibility of healthcare, aligning with the core objectives of healthcare stewardship.

The financial performance of healthcare organizations can benefit from the integration of ESG and stewardship principles. Sustainable practices often lead to cost savings through reduced energy consumption, medical and non-medical waste management efficiencies, and optimized resource use. These savings can be reinvested into patient care and infrastructure improvements, enhancing the overall quality of healthcare services. ESG-aligned organizations may also attract investment from socially responsible investors who prioritize long-term sustainability and ethical, empirically-supported healthcare management. This financial support can provide the capital needed to implement further advancements in healthcare delivery, creating a virtuous cycle of improvement and sustainability.

In summary, the relationship between ESG and healthcare stewardship is mutually reinforcing, with each framework supporting and enhancing the other. Environmental sustainability, social responsibility and equity, and strong governance and leadership are integral to the responsible management of healthcare resources. By integrating ESG principles into healthcare stewardship, organizations can ensure that they are meeting their ethical obligations to patients and communities while also contributing to the broader goals of sustainability, collective impact, and social justice. This holistic, integrated, and comprehensive approach is essential for building resilient and equitable healthcare systems capable of addressing the complex challenges of the 21st century.

9.6 REFERENCES

Barna, S., Maric, F., Simons, J., et al. (2020) Education for the Anthropocene: Planetary health, sustainable health care, and the health workforce.*Medical Teacher*42 (10): 1091-1096.

Bhattacharya, A., Bhattacharya, S. (2023) Integrating ESG pillars for business model innovation in the biopharmaceutical industry. *Australasian Accounting, Business and Finance Journal* 17 (1): 127-150.

Buse, C. G., Oestreicher, J. S., Ellis, N. R., et al. (2018) Public health guide to field developments linking ecosystems, environments and health in the Anthropocene.*J Epidemiol Community Health*72 (5): 420-425.

Churet, C., Eccles, R. G. (2014) Integrated reporting, quality of management, and financial performance.*Journal of Applied Corporate Finance*26 (1): 56-64.

Davis, D., Krupnick, A., Thurston, G. (2000) The ancillary health benefits and costs of GHG mitigation: scope, scale, and credibility. *In*Ancillary Benefits and Costs of Greenhouse Gas Mitigation: Proceedings of an IPCC Co-sponsored Workshop (pp. 135-190).

Feist, T. (2018) The Three Scopes of Greenhouse Gas Emissions.*Journal of Property Management* 83 (3): 24-26.

Folke, C., Carpenter, S. R., Chapin III, F. S., et al. (2020) Our Future in the Anthropocene Biosphere: Global sustainability and resilient societies.

Ghaemi, Z., Smith, A. D. (2020) A review on the quantification of life cycle greenhouse gas emissions at urban scale.*Journal of Cleaner Production* 252: 119634.

Iyiola, A. O., Babafemi, O. P., Ogundahunsi, O. E., et al. (2022) Food security: a pathway towards improved nutrition and biodiversity conservation. *In*Biodiversity in Africa: Potentials, Threats and Conservation(pp. 79-107). Singapore: Springer Nature Singapore.

Kareiva, P., Fuller, E. (2016) Beyond resilience: how to better prepare for the profound disruption of the Anthropocene.*Global Policy* 7: 107-118.

Khasim, S. M., Long, C., Thammasiri, K., et al. (Eds.). (2020)*Medicinal plants: biodiversity, sustainable utilization and conservation.* Singapore: Springer.

Lafferty, K. D. (2009) The ecology of climate change and infectious diseases.*Ecology* 90 (4): 888-900.

Leung, T. C. H., You, C. S. X. (2023) ESG Application in Sustainable Development of the Healthcare Industry. *In*Environmental, Social and Governance and Sustainable Development in Healthcare(pp. 47-64). Singapore: Springer Nature Singapore.

McLean, M., Behrens, G., Chase, et al. (2022) The medical education planetary health journey: advancing the agenda in the health professions requires eco-ethical leadership and inclusive collaboration.*Challenges*13 (2): 62.

Morand, S., Walther, B. A. (2020) The accelerated infectious disease risk in the Anthropocene: more outbreaks and wider global spread.*BioR.*

Mostepaniuk, A., Akalin, T., Parish, M. R. (2023) Practices pursuing the sustainability of a healthcare organization: A systematic review.*Sustainability*15 (3): 2353.

National Academies of Sciences, Engineering, and Medicine Division,& Committee on Integrating Social Needs Care into the Delivery of Health Care to Improve the Nation's Health. (2019) Integrating social care into the delivery of health care: Moving upstream to improve the nation's health.

Nakielski, M. L. (2023) Moving Forward with ESG, Sustainability, and Corporate Responsibility.*Frontiers of Health Services Management*40 (1): 33-39.

Roka, K. (2020) Anthropocene and climate change.*Climate Action* 20-32.

Sasser, J. S. (2018) Public health in the anthropocene: Exploring population fears and climate threats. *In*Global Health and Security(pp. 166-178). Routledge.

Sepetis, A., Rizos, F., Pierrakos, G., et al. (2024) A sustainable model for healthcare systems: The innovative approach of ESG and digital transformation. *Healthcare*12 (2): 156.

Sharma, I., Birman, S. (2024) Biodiversity Loss, Ecosystem Services, and Their Role in Promoting Sustainable Health. *In*The Climate-Health-Sustainability Nexus: Understanding the Interconnected Impact on Populations and the Environment(pp. 163-188). Cham: Springer Nature Switzerland.

Shaw, E., Walpole, S., McLean, M., et al. (2021) AMEE Consensus Statement: Planetary health and education for sustainable healthcare.*Medical Teacher* 43 (3): 272-286.

Tong, S., Bambrick, H., Beggs, P. J., et al. (2022) Current and future threats to human health in the Anthropocene.*Environment international*158: 106892.

World Health Organization. (2021) Nature, biodiversity and health: an overview of interconnections.

CHAPTER 10

ANTI-MICROBIAL STEWARDSHIP: A MULTI-LEVEL GLOBAL BURNING PLATFORM IN HEALTHCARE STEWARDSHIP AND SUSTAINABILITY

10.1 THE BURNING PLATFORM IN THE CONTEXT OF HEALTHCARE

The term *burning platform* is a metaphor used in business to describe a situation where someone must make a drastic change in their behavior to avoid dire consequences.It comes from the true story of Andy Mochan, a worker on the Piper Alpha oil rig in the North Sea when it exploded in July 1988 (Conner, 1992).The explosion caused a massive fire that killed 167 men, and Mochan was awakened and faced a choice to either stay on the platform and burn alive or jump into the freezing water. Mochan chose to jump and survived, and later said that the experience caused a radical change in his behavior. In business, the concept of a *burning platform* is used to help people see the consequences of not changing and motivate them to embrace change.However, some say that overuse of the term can dilute the alignment needed to succeed, and that people can become numb and dismissive if there is a constant series of *burning platforms*.

In the general context of healthcare management (Warner et al., 2015), the *burning platform* refers to the critical and pressing issues that necessitate immediate and decisive action to prevent catastrophic health outcomes.

One critical *burning platform* in healthcare is the chronic shortage of healthcare professionals, exacerbated by the COVID-19 pandemic (Teixeria, 2020) This shortage created a cascade of problems, including increased workloads for existing staff, potential compromises in patient care quality and safety, and higher operational costs due to the reliance on temporary staffing solutions. The stress and burnout experienced by healthcare workers further amplified the crisis, leading to higher turnover rates and a continuous cycle of staffing challenges. Addressing this burning platform required a multilayered and interdisciplinary approach, including strategic workforce development, improved working conditions, investment in education and training programs, and policies that support the retention and well-being of healthcare professionals.

The financial sustainability of healthcare systems is also a burning platform that demands urgent attention (Patel et al., 2019). Rising healthcare costs, driven by factors such as an aging population, advancements in medical technology, and the increasing prevalence of chronic diseases, place immense pressure on healthcare budgets. This financial strain can lead to difficult choices about resource allocation and may compromise the ability to provide high-quality care to all patients. Implementing value-based models of care that focus on delivering high-quality outcomes at lower costs is essential to address this burning platform. These care models emphasize the integration of holistic and comprehensive evidence-based care, patient engagement, and the use of data to drive efficient and effective healthcare delivery to best practices.

Healthcare disparities and inequities represent yet another burning platform that calls for immediate action (Dickman et al., 2017).

Upstream socioeconomic factors, geographic location, race, and ethnicity significantly influence access and navigation to healthcare services. These disparities have been bluntly highlighted by the COVID-19 pandemic, which disproportionately affected marginalized and underserved communities. To address this burning platform, healthcare systems must adopt strategies that promote equity, such as expanding access to care where people live, play and work, implementing culturally competent clinicians and *bricks and mortar* sites of care, and addressing the upstream determinants of health. Ensuring that all individuals receive just and equitable treatment is not only a moral and ethical imperative but also essential for improving the public's health, wellness, and well-being.

The burning platforms in the context of healthcare delivery represent imperative matters that require immediate and decisive action to prevent catastrophic outcomes. Whether it is the threat of antibiotic resistance, the healthcare workforce crisis, financial sustainability, or healthcare disparities, each of these challenges demands a strategic and coordinated response. By recognizing and addressing these burning platforms, healthcare systems can safeguard public health, ensure the delivery of high-quality care, and build a more resilient and equitable healthcare infrastructure for the future.

10.2 ANTI-MICROBIAL STEWARDSHIP: THE NEXT BURNING PLATFORM?

Antimicrobial stewardship is considered a burning platform due to the immediate and severe threat posed by antibiotic resistance, which endangers global public health and the efficacy of modern medicine (Birgand et al., 2023; Frieri et al., 2017). The rapid emergence and spread of multidrug-resistant organisms significantly limit treatment options for infections, making once easily treatable illnesses potentially lethal. The urgency to address this issue cannot be overstated, as the continued misuse and overuse of antibiotics accelerate the development of resistance, leading to a scenario where common infections could become untreatable, and routine surgeries and medical procedures carry a higher risk of complications and mortality.

The economic impact of antibiotic resistance further underscores its status as a burning platform (Ahmad et al., 2019). Treating infections caused by resistant organisms is substantially more expensive than treating those caused by susceptible strains, due to the need for more complex, prolonged, and costly treatments. This financial burden affects not only individual patients but also healthcare systems and economies worldwide. Increased healthcare costs, longer hospital stays, and the need for more intensive care contribute to a strain on healthcare resources, making it imperative to implement effective antimicrobial stewardship programs to curb the economic drain caused by antibiotic resistance.

Patient safety is also at the heart of why antimicrobial stewardship is a burning platform (Domer et al., 2021). Inappropriate use of antibiotics can lead to adverse drug reactions, including life-threatening conditions such as <u>Clostridium difficile</u> infections, which often result from disrupted gut microbiota. These infections are difficult to treat and can cause severe morbidity and mortality, particularly in vulnerable populations such as the elderly and immunocompromised patients. Ensuring the appropriate use of antibiotics through stewardship programs helps prevent these adverse outcomes, safeguarding patient health and improving overall clinical outcomes.

Moreover, the global nature of antibiotic resistance exacerbates its urgency (Aljeldah, 2022). Resistant pathogens do not respect borders, and the misuse of antibiotics in one part of the world can have far-reaching consequences, spreading resistance internationally. This interconnectedness necessitates a coordinated and comprehensive response, involving international collaboration and adherence to stewardship principles across all healthcare settings. The failure to address antibiotic resistance on a global scale could lead to a public health crisis of unprecedented proportions, similar to the SARS-CoV-2 viral pandemic (i.e., COVID-19) of 2020, making antimicrobial stewardship an immediate priority.

Antimicrobial stewardship is considered a burning platform due to the calamitous and immediate consequences of international, national, and local antibiotic resistance for public health, economic stability, patient safety, and healthcare delivery systems. The urgent need to preserve the effectiveness of existing antibiotics and develop sustainable practices for their use underscores the critical importance of robust stewardship programs. Addressing this burning platform through concerted efforts can help prevent a future where common infections become deadly and modern medical practices are severely compromised.

10.3 ANTI-MICROBIAL STEWARDSHIP IS FOUNDATIONAL TO THE AMERICAN HEALTHCARE DELIVERY SYSTEM

Antimicrobial stewardship is foundational to the US healthcare delivery system for several significant reasons: it helps combat antibiotic resistance, ensures effective patient care, and protects the public's health, wellness and well-being. (Logan et al., 2019; Hwang et al., 2021).

Antibiotic resistance is one of the most pressing public health threats globally (Ferri et al., 2017; Dhingra et al., 2020). Misuse and overuse of antibiotics accelerate the development of resistant bacteria, rendering standard treatments ineffective. This leads to infections that are harder to treat, increasing morbidity, mortality, and healthcare costs. Antimicrobial stewardship aims to optimize antibiotic use to slow the emergence of resistance, ensuring that these life-saving drugs remain effective for future generations.

Effective antimicrobial stewardship ensures that patients receive the right antibiotic, at the right dose, for the right duration (Bankar et al., 2022). This targeted approach reduces the likelihood of adverse drug reactions and secondary infections, such as Clostridioides difficile, which can be caused by broad-spectrum antibiotic use. By promoting precise and appropriate antibiotic use, stewardship programs enhance patient safety and improve overall clinical outcomes.

Infections caused by resistant organisms are more challenging and expensive to treat (Laxminarayan et al., 2016; Sipahi, 2008). They often require longer hospital stays, more intensive care, and more expensive and toxic drugs. By preventing the development and spread of resistance, antimicrobial stewardship helps contain healthcare costs. Additionally, reducing unnecessary antibiotic use minimizes the risk of costly adverse drug events and secondary infections.

The development of new antibiotics is slow and expensive, and the pipeline for new drugs is limited (Ardal et al., 2020). Stewardship programs play a critical role in preserving the effectiveness of existing antibiotics by promoting their judicious use. This is essential for maintaining the ability to treat bacterial infections effectively and for ensuring that antibiotics remain a viable option in the future.

Antimicrobial stewardship works hand in hand with infection prevention and control measures (Giamarellou et al., 2023). By reducing unnecessary antibiotic use, stewardship programs help decrease the prevalence of resistant bacteria within healthcare settings. This, in turn, reduces the risk of hospital-acquired infections and the spread of resistant organisms to vulnerable patient populations.

Antimicrobial stewardship is a cornerstone of public health efforts to combat antibiotic resistance (Hwang et al., 2021; Tamma et al., 2011; Owens, 2008). National and international health organizations, such as the Centers for Disease Control and Prevention (CDC) and the World Health Organization (WHO), emphasize the importance of stewardship programs in their essential public health strategies, services, and functions to address resistance. These programs align with broader public health goals to improve healthcare quality and safety, protect vulnerable populations, and promote sustainable antibiotic use practices.

Stewardship programs play a vital role in educating healthcare providers about appropriate antibiotic prescribing practices and the importance of resistance. They also help inform patients about the proper use of antibiotics and the risks associated with misuse. This education fosters a culture of responsible antibiotic use and enhances the overall effectiveness of antimicrobial stewardship efforts (Lim et al., 2020; Ancillotti et al., 2018).

Antimicrobial stewardship is essential for addressing the critical threat of antibiotic resistance, improving patient outcomes, reducing healthcare costs, preserving the efficacy of current antibiotics, enhancing infection control, supporting public health initiatives, and educating both healthcare providers and patients. Through multi-layered and interdisciplinary efforts, stewardship programs play a pivotal role in safeguarding the public's health, wellness, and well-being and by actively pursuing the sustainable use of antibiotics.

10.4 ANTI-MICROBIAL STEWARDSHIP, THE AMERICAN HEALTHCARE DELIVERY SYSTEM, AND EVIDENCE-BASED BEST CLINICAL PRACTICE.

Antimicrobial stewardship in the American healthcare delivery system is an essential strategy aimed at optimizing the use of antimicrobial agents to combat the growing threat of antibiotic resistance (Kapadia et al., 2018; Weinstein et al., 2022; Lane et al., 2019). This initiative focuses on ensuring that patients receive the most appropriate antibiotic therapy, including the correct drug, dose, and duration of treatment, while minimizing the potential for adverse effects and the development of resistance. By implementing evidence-based guidelines and protocols, healthcare providers can improve patient outcomes, reduce the incidence of infections caused by multidrug-resistant organisms, and preserve the efficacy of existing antibiotics for future generations, i.e., practicing the principles of healthcare stewardship and sustainability.

Central to antimicrobial stewardship is the collaboration among various healthcare professionals, including physicians, pharmacists, nurses, and infection prevention specialists (Barlam, 2021). This multidisciplinary approach ensures a comprehensive review of antibiotic use and promotes the adoption of best clinical practice guidelines across all levels of care. Electronic health records and clinical decision support systems play a crucial role in facilitating these efforts by providing real-time data on antibiotic prescribing patterns, resistance trends, and patient outcomes. Furthermore, ongoing education and training for healthcare providers are vital to maintaining awareness and adherence to stewardship principles (Dikkatwar et al., 2024).

Public health agencies, such as the Centers for Disease Control and Prevention (CDC), have been instrumental in advancing antimicrobial stewardship efforts in the United States. Through initiatives like the National Healthcare Safety Network (Classen et al., 2024) and the Antibiotic Resistance Solutions Initiative (Joshi et al., 2023), the CDC provides guidance, resources, and support to healthcare facilities nationwide. These programs help track progress, identify areas for improvement, and promote the widespread adoption of stewardship practices. Additionally, policy initiatives at the federal and state levels have been crucial in establishing regulatory frameworks that encourage and mandate stewardship activities (Cosgrove et al., 2024).

Patient engagement is another critical component of effective antimicrobial stewardship. Educating patients about the appropriate use of antibiotics, the risks associated with misuse, and the importance of adhering to prescribed treatment regimens can significantly impact their behavior and attitudes toward antibiotics. By fostering a better understanding of antibiotic resistance and the role of stewardship, healthcare providers can empower patients to participate actively in their care and make informed decisions about their treatment (Van Dort, 2024).

Antimicrobial stewardship in the American healthcare delivery system is a multilayered interdisciplinary approach that involves the concerted efforts of healthcare professionals, public health agencies, policymakers, and patients. By optimizing antibiotic use, reducing resistance, and improving patient outcomes, antimicrobial stewardship programs are essential to ensuring the long-term efficacy of antimicrobial agents and safeguarding public health. The continued advancement and expansion of these initiatives are critical to addressing the challenges posed by antibiotic resistance and maintaining the integrity of the healthcare system.

10.5 CHALLENGES TO IMPLEMENTING ANTI-MICROBIAL STEWARDSHIP INTO HEALTHCARE SYSTEMS

Implementing effective antimicrobial stewardship programs in the American healthcare delivery system presents several significant challenges. One of the primary obstacles is the variability in resources and infrastructure across different healthcare settings (Vaughn et al., 2024). Smaller hospitals and rural clinics often lack the necessary personnel, technology, and funding to establish and maintain robust stewardship programs. This disparity creates an uneven landscape where the quality of antibiotic management can vary widely, potentially undermining broader efforts to combat antibiotic resistance.

Another challenge lies in the complexity of changing established prescribing behaviors among healthcare providers (Powers, 2024). Many physicians and clinicians have long-standing habits and practices that may not align with current stewardship guidelines. Overcoming these ingrained behaviors requires continuous education, training, and the implementation of effective clinical decision support tools. However, ensuring consistent adherence to these guidelines across diverse and busy healthcare environments is difficult, especially when immediate clinical pressures and patient demands can influence decision-making.

The need for accurate and timely data is also a significant hurdle (Howard et al., 2024). Effective antimicrobial stewardship relies heavily on a learning health system framework for real-time data regarding antibiotic prescribing patterns, resistance trends, and patient outcomes. Many healthcare facilities struggle with integrating comprehensive data collection and analytic systems into their workflows. Without truthful and reliable data, monitoring and evaluating the impact of stewardship interventions becomes challenging, making it difficult to identify areas for improvement and measure success.

Alignment between antimicrobial stewardship goals and broader organizational priorities is often lacking (Ohlsen et al., 2024). Healthcare institutions are frequently under pressure to achieve financial targets, meet regulatory requirements, and manage patient throughput. In such an environment, stewardship initiatives can be perceived as secondary or even burdensome, leading to insufficient support from leadership. Ensuring that antimicrobial stewardship is recognized as a critical component of overall patient safety and quality of care requires strong advocacy and clear communication of its long-term benefits.

Patient expectations and misconceptions about antibiotics present another layer of complexity (Dikkatwar et al., 2024). Many patients expect or demand antibiotics for conditions that do not require them, such as viral infections. Educating patients about the appropriate use of antibiotics and the risks of overuse and misuse is essential, but changing public perception and behavior is a slow and ongoing process. Healthcare providers must balance patient satisfaction with the principles of stewardship, often navigating difficult conversations to avoid unnecessary antibiotic prescriptions.

Antimicrobial stewardship in the American healthcare delivery system faces significant challenges, including resource variability, fixed provider prescribing behaviors, data integration issues, organizational alignment, and patient misconceptions. Addressing these challenges requires a multifaceted approach, including sustained education, robust data systems, strong leadership support, and ongoing public engagement. Overcoming these obstacles is crucial to advancing stewardship efforts and combating the growing threat of antibiotic resistance.

10.6 INFECTION PREVENTION AND CONTROL: ANTI-MICROBIAL STEWARDSHIP IN ACTION

Infection prevention and control (IPC) is a fundamental aspect of healthcare that aims to protect patients, healthcare workers, and the community from the spread of infectious diseases (Tartari et al., 2021; Alhumaid et al., 2021; Billings et al., 2019).

Effective IPC practices are essential for reducing the incidence of healthcare-associated infections (HAIs), which can lead to serious complications, prolonged hospital stays, and increased healthcare costs. These practices include a combination of measures such as hand hygiene, the use of personal protective equipment (PPE), environmental cleaning, sterilization of medical equipment, and isolation protocols. By implementing robust IPC programs, healthcare facilities can create safer environments, improve patient outcomes, and minimize the transmission of infections.

Hand hygiene is a cornerstone of infection prevention and control (Mouajou et al., 2022). Proper handwashing with soap and water or the use of alcohol-based hand sanitizers is one of the most effective ways to prevent the spread of pathogens. Healthcare workers must adhere to strict hand hygiene protocols before and after patient contact, after contact with potentially contaminated surfaces, and before performing any aseptic tasks. Ensuring compliance with hand hygiene guidelines requires continuous education, monitoring, and feedback. In addition, providing adequate hand hygiene facilities and supplies is critical to supporting this vital practice.

The use of personal protective equipment (PPE) is another key component of IPC. PPE includes items such as gloves, masks, gowns, and face shields, which provide a barrier against infectious agents. The appropriate selection and use of PPE depend on the nature of the patient interaction and the type of infection being managed. Training healthcare workers on the correct donning and doffing techniques is essential to prevent self-contamination and the spread of pathogens. The COVID-19 pandemic has highlighted the importance of PPE in protecting healthcare workers and controlling the spread of respiratory infections, underscoring the need for adequate PPE supplies and proper usage protocols (Janson et. al., 2022; Liu, 2024)

Environmental cleaning and disinfection are critical for reducing the transmission of infections within healthcare settings. Pathogens can survive on surfaces for extended periods, making regular cleaning and disinfection of patient rooms, common areas, and medical equipment essential. IPC programs must establish comprehensive cleaning protocols that specify the frequency and methods of cleaning, as well as the types of disinfectants to be used (Edward et. al., 2024). Training housekeeping staff and ensuring adherence to these protocols are crucial for maintaining a hygienic environment and preventing the spread of infections.

Sterilization and disinfection of medical equipment are also vital to IPC (Thakur et al., 2024). Reusable medical instruments and devices must be properly cleaned, disinfected, or sterilized according to established guidelines to prevent cross-contamination between patients. Sterilization processes, such as autoclaving, and high-level disinfection methods are used to eliminate all forms of microbial life, including spores. Healthcare facilities must implement stringent protocols for the handling, processing, and storage of sterile equipment to ensure its safety and effectiveness.

Isolation protocols are necessary for managing patients with contagious infections (Blackwell, 2024). These protocols involve isolating infected patients to prevent the spread of pathogens to other patients, healthcare workers, and visitors. Different types of isolation, such as contact, droplet, and airborne precautions, are employed based on the mode of transmission of the infectious agent. Implementing isolation measures requires proper patient placement, use of PPE, and strict adherence to hand hygiene and environmental cleaning practices. Effective communication and coordination among healthcare team members are essential to successfully manage isolation cases.

In conclusion, infection prevention and control are integral to maintaining the health, safety, and welfare of patients, healthcare workers, and the community. By adhering to rigorous hand-hygiene practices, utilizing appropriate PPE, ensuring thorough environmental cleaning, properly sterilizing medical equipment, and implementing isolation protocols, healthcare facilities can significantly reduce the risk of hospital-acquired infections and limit the spread of infectious diseases. Strong IPC programs, supported by continuous education, training, and compliance monitoring, are crucial for achieving these goals and fostering a culture of safety and accountability in the delivery of healthcare services.

10.7 THE FUTURE OF ANTI-MICROBIAL STEWARDSHIP IN THE US

The future of antimicrobial stewardship in the United States is poised to be shaped by a combination of technological advancements, policy initiatives, and evolving healthcare practices. With the growing threat of antibiotic resistance, which poses a significant public health risk, there is an increasing emphasis on optimizing the use of antimicrobials (Cocker et al., 2024). This involves not only prescribing the right antibiotics when necessary but also minimizing unnecessary usage. As such, the future will likely see a more robust implementation of stewardship programs across healthcare settings, including hospitals, outpatient clinics, and long-term care facilities. These programs will focus on improving diagnostic accuracy, enhancing infection control and prevention measures, and promoting the use of narrow-spectrum antibiotics to preserve the efficacy of broad-spectrum options (Williams et al., 2024).

Technological innovations, such as rapid diagnostic tests and advanced data analytics, will play a crucial role in the evolution of antimicrobial stewardship (Bonello et al., 2024). Rapid diagnostics can help healthcare providers quickly identify the pathogens causing infections and determine their susceptibility to various antibiotics, allowing for more targeted and effective treatment. Additionally, the integration of electronic health records (EHRs) with decision-support tools can provide real-time alerts and recommendations to clinicians, ensuring adherence to best clinical practice guidelines (White et al., 2023). The use of big data, machine learning, and artificial intelligence can also enable the analysis of prescribing patterns and resistance trends, helping to refine stewardship strategies and track their impact over time (de la Lastra et al., 2024; Harry, 2024).

Public policy and regulatory frameworks will continue to be key drivers in advancing antimicrobial stewardship efforts (Cosgrove et al., 2023). The Centers for Disease Control and Prevention (CDC) and other governmental bodies at all levels of organization are likely to implement more stringent regulations and incentives to encourage the adoption of stewardship practices. This may include mandatory reporting of antibiotic use and resistance data, as well as financial incentives for healthcare facilities that demonstrate effective stewardship programs. Additionally, public education campaigns will be critical in raising awareness about the appropriate use of antibiotics among patients and the general public, thereby reducing the demand for unnecessary prescriptions (Parveen et al., 2022).

The future of antimicrobial stewardship in the US will also be shaped by a more collaborative approach across various sectors, including healthcare, agriculture, and veterinary medicine (Zinsstag et al., 2021). The One Health framework, which recognizes the interconnectedness of human, animal, and environmental health, will become increasingly important in addressing the issue of antibiotic resistance comprehensively. This integrated approach will involve coordinated efforts to monitor and control antibiotic use in agriculture, where overuse and misuse can contribute to the development of resistant bacteria that can spread to humans through food ingestion.

Overall, the future of antimicrobial stewardship in the United States is likely to be characterized by a more proactive, data-driven, and multidisciplinary approach. By leveraging technological advancements, policy measures, and collaborative efforts, the goal will be to preserve the efficacy of existing antibiotics, develop new treatment options, and ultimately safeguard public health against the growing threat of antibiotic resistance.

10.8 REFERENCES

Ahmad, M., Khan, A. U. (2019) Global economic impact of antibiotic resistance: A review. *Journal of Global Antimicrobial Resistance* 19: 313-316.

Alhumaid, S., Al Mutair, A., Al Alawi, Z., et al. (2021) Knowledge of infection prevention and control among healthcare workers and factors influencing compliance: a systematic review. *Antimicrobial Resistance& Infection Control*10 (1): 86.

Aljeldah, M. M. (2022) Antimicrobial resistance and its spread is a global threat.*Antibiotics* 11 (8): 1082.

Ancillotti, M., Eriksson, S., Veldwijk, J., et al. (2018) Public awareness and individual responsibility needed for judicious use of antibiotics: a qualitative study of public beliefs and perceptions. *BMC Public Health*18: 1-9.

Årdal, C., Balasegaram, M., Laxminarayan, et al. (2020) Antibiotic development—economic, regulatory and societal challenges. *Nature Reviews Microbiology*18 (5): 267-274.

Bankar, N. J., Ugemuge, S., Ambad, et al. (2022). Implementation of antimicrobial stewardship in the healthcare setting.*Cureus*14 (7).

Barlam, T. F. (2021) The state of antibiotic stewardship programs in 2021: The perspective of an experienced steward.*Antimicrobial Stewardship& Healthcare Epidemiology*1 (1): e20.

Birgand, G., Dhar, P., Holmes, A. (2023) The threat of antimicrobial resistance in surgical care: the surgeon's role and ownership of antimicrobial stewardship.*British Journal of Surgery*110 (12): 1567-1569.

Billings, C., Bernard, H., Caffery, L., et al. (2019) Advancing the profession: An updated future-oriented competency model for professional development in infection prevention and control. *American Journal of Infection Control*47 (6): 602-614.

Blackwell, C. W. (2024) Application of the Centers for Disease Control and Prevention's isolation directives for patients exposed to severe acute respiratory syndrome coronavirus 2.*The Journal for Nurse Practitioners*20 (4): 104962.

Bonello, M., Applegate, T. L., Badman, S., et al. (2024) The AMR Hub: a public–private partnership to overcome barriers to commercialisation and deliver antimicrobial stewardship innovations.*Microbiology Australia.*

Classen, D. C., Rhee, C., Dantes, R. B., et al. (2024) Healthcare-associated infections and conditions in the era of digital measurement.*Infection Control& Hospital Epidemiology*45 (1): 3-8.

Cocker, D., Birgand, G., Zhu, N., et al. (2024) Healthcare as a driver, reservoir and amplifier of antimicrobial resistance: opportunities for interventions.*Nature Reviews Microbiology* pp 1-14.

Conner, D. R. (1992) *Managing at the Speed of Change: How Resilient Managers Succeed and Prosper Where Others Fail.* Villard Books.

Cosgrove, S. E., Ahn, R., Dullabh, P., et al. (2024) Lessons Learned from a National Hospital Antibiotic Stewardship Implementation Project.*The Joint Commission Journal on Quality and Patient Safety* 50 (6): 435-441.

Cosgrove, S. E., Srinivasan, A. (2023) Antibiotic stewardship: a decade of progress.*Infectious Disease Clinics*37 (4): 659-667.

de la Lastra, J. M. P., Wardell, S. J., Pal, T., et al. (2024) From Data to Decisions: Leveraging Artificial Intelligence and Machine Learning in Combating Antimicrobial Resistance–a Comprehensive Review.*Journal of Medical Systems*48 (1): 71.

Dhingra, S., Rahman, N. A. A., Peile, E., et al. (2020) Microbial resistance movements: an overview of global public health threats posed by antimicrobial resistance, and how best to counter.*Frontiers in Public Health*8: 535668.

Dickman, S. L., Himmelstein, D. U., Woolhandler, S. (2017) Inequality and the health-care system in the USA.*The Lancet*389 (10077): 1431-1441.

Dikkatwar, M. S., Chand, S., Varghese, et al. (2024) Antimicrobial stewardship: smart approach to combat antibiotic resistance. *Anti-infective Agents*22 (4): 23-31.

Domer, G., Gallagher, T. M., Shahabzada, S., et al. (2021) Patient safety: preventing patient harm and building capacity for patient safety. *In*Contemporary Topics in Patient Safety-Volume 1. Intech Open.

Edward, M., John, W., Mahulu, E., et al. (2024) Challenges of Compliance with Infection Prevention and Control (IPC) Standard Procedures among Healthcare Workers: A Hospital-Based Cross-Sectional Study.*International Journal of Health Policy Planning*3 (1): 1-7.

Ferri, M., Ranucci, E., Romagnoli, P., et al. (2017) Antimicrobial resistance: A global emerging threat to public health systems. *Critical Reviews in Food Science and Nutrition*57 (13): 2857-2876.

Frieri, M., Kumar, K., Boutin, A. (2017) Antibiotic resistance.*Journal of Infection and Public Health* 10 (4): 369-378.

Giamarellou, H., Galani, L., Karavasilis, T., et al. (2023) Antimicrobial stewardship in the hospital setting: a narrative review. *Antibiotics*12 (10): 1557.

Harry, A. (2024) Revolutionizing Healthcare: The Role of Artificial Intelligence in Antibiotic Stewardship and Resistance Management.*International Journal of Multidisciplinary Sciences and Arts*3 (1): 325-332.

Howard, A., Aston, S., Gerada, A., et al. (2024) Antimicrobial learning systems: an implementation blueprint for artificial intelligence to tackle antimicrobial resistance.*The Lancet Digital Health* 6 (1): e79-e86.

Hwang, S., Kwon, K. T. (2021). Core elements for successful implementation of antimicrobial stewardship programs. *Infection& Chemotherapy*53 (3), 421.

Janson, D. J., Clift, B. C., Dhokia, V. (2022) PPE fit of healthcare workers during the COVID-19 pandemic. *Applied Ergonomics* 99: 103610.

Joshi, P., Bajpai, D. K. 2023 Antibiotic resistance: overuse of antibiotics, context and potential solutions. *IJTI* 1 (2): viii-xv.

Kapadia, S. N., Abramson, E. L., Carter, E. J., et al. (2018) The expanding role of antimicrobial stewardship programs in hospitals in the United States: lessons learned from a multisite qualitative study. *The Joint Commission Journal on Quality and Patient Safety* 44 (2): 68-74.

Lane, M. A., Hays, A. J., Newland, H., et al. (2019) Development of an antimicrobial stewardship program in an integrated healthcare system. *American Journal of Health-System Pharmacy* 76 (1): 34-43.

Laxminarayan, R., Matsoso, P., Pant, S., et al. (2016) Access to effective antimicrobials: a worldwide challenge. *The Lancet* 387 (10014): 168-175.

Lim, J. M., Singh, S. R., Duong, M. C., et al. (2020) Impact of national interventions to promote responsible antibiotic use: a systematic review. *Journal of Antimicrobial Chemotherapy* 75 (1): 14-29.

Liu, C. (2024) PPE-Based Strategies For COVID-19 Prevention Amongst Healthcare Workers. *Highlights in Science, Engineering and Technology* 102: 709-717.

Logan, A. Y., Williamson, J. E., Reinke, et al. (2019) Establishing an antimicrobial stewardship collaborative across a large, diverse health care system. *The Joint Commission Journal on Quality and Patient Safety* 45 (9): 591-599.

Mouajou, V., Adams, K., DeLisle, G., et al. (2022). Hand hygiene compliance in the prevention of hospital-acquired infections: a systematic review. *Journal of Hospital Infection* 119: 33-48.

Ohlsen, J. T., Søfteland, E., Akselsen, P. E., et al. (2024). Rapid response systems, antibiotic stewardship and medication reconciliation: a scoping review on implementation factors, activities and outcomes.*BMJ Quality& Safety.*

Owens Jr, R. C. (2008) Antimicrobial stewardship: concepts and strategies in the 21st century.*Diagnostic Microbiology and Infectious Disease*61 (1): 110-128.

Parveen, S., Garzon-Orjuela, N., Amin, D., et al. (2022) Public health interventions to improve antimicrobial resistance awareness and behavioural change associated with antimicrobial use: a systematic review exploring the use of social media.*Antibiotics*11 (5): 669.

Patel, K., Rushefsky, M. E. (2019)*Healthcare politics and policy in America*. Routledge.

Powers, J. H. (2024). Antimicrobial stewardship.*BMJ*385.

Sipahi, O. R. (2008) Economics of antibiotic resistance.*Expert Review of Anti-infective Therapy*6 (4): 523-539.

Tamma, P. D., Cosgrove, S. E. (2011) Antimicrobial stewardship. *Infectious Disease Clinics*25 (1): 245-260.

Tartari, E., Tomczyk, S., Pires, D., et al. (2021). Implementation of the infection prevention and control core components at the national level: a global situational analysis.*Journal of Hospital Infection*108: 94-103.

Teixeira, C. F. D. S., Soares, C. M., Souza, E. A., et al. (2020) The health of healthcare professionals coping with the Covid-19 pandemic.Ciencia& Saude Coletiva25: 3465-3474.

Thakur, H., Rao, R. (2024) Emphasis of infection prevention and control: a review.*J Popul Therap Clin Pharmacol* 31: 2238-49.

Van Dort, B. A. (2024)*An in-depth exploration of antimicrobial stewardship: The interplay between people and systems.* University of Sydney Doctoral Dissertation.

Vaughn, V. M., Krein, S. L., Hersh, A. L., et al. (2024) Excellence in Antibiotic Stewardship: A Mixed-Methods Study Comparing High-, Medium-, and Low-Performing Hospitals.*Clinical Infectious Diseases* 78 (6): 1412-1424.

Warner, M. A., Apfelbaum, J. L. (2015) The perioperative surgical home: a response to a presumed burning platform or a thoughtful expansion of anesthesiology?*Anesthesia& Analgesia*120 (5): 1149-1151.

Weinstein, R. Buckel, W. R., Stenehjem, E. A., et al. (2022) Harnessing the power of health systems and networks for antimicrobial stewardship.*Clinical Infectious Diseases* 75 (11): 2038-2044.

White, N. M., Carter, H. E., Kularatna, S., et al. (2023) Evaluating the costs and consequences of computerized clinical decision support systems in hospitals: a scoping review and recommendations for future practice.*Journal of the American Medical Informatics Association*30 (6): 1205-1218.

Williams, S. B., McCaffrey, P., Reynoso, D., et al. (2024) Implementation of a High-Value, Evidence-Based Care Program: Impact and Opportunities for Learning Organizations.*Journal of Healthcare Management*69 (4): 296-308.

Zinsstag, J., Schelling, E., Crump, L., et al. (eds.) (2021)*One Health: the theory and practice of integrated health approaches.* CABI.

CHAPTER 11

THE FUTURE OF SUSTAINABLE HEALTHCARE STEWARDSHIP

11.1 THE FUTURE OF HEALTHCARE STEWARDSHIP IN 21ST CENTURY HEALTHCARE

The future of healthcare stewardship will be influenced by various factors, such as technological advancements, demographic shifts, and changing societal expectations. As healthcare systems worldwide face the mounting challenges of aging populations, rising healthcare costs, and the constant threat of pandemics, responsible, effective, empirically supported, and evidence-based health management will become ever more essential for ensuring the health, wellness, and well-being of future generations.

The integration of innovative technologies, such as artificial intelligence (AI), telemedicine, and big data analytics, offers significant potential to enhance the efficiency and effectiveness of healthcare delivery (Maleki-Vamosfaderani et al., 2024). By leveraging these tools, healthcare systems can improve equitable resource allocation, streamline operations, and personalize patient care, ultimately leading to better health outcomes and more sustainable healthcare systems.

In the coming years, healthcare stewardship will need to increasingly focus on population health management, people-centered care, and value-based approaches to resource utilization, with the goal of improving quality and reducing the overall cost of care. This shift requires a more proactive approach, focusing on health prevention, promotion, protection, and preparedness with early detection and management of both communicable and non-communicable chronic diseases. Healthy public policies and practices, like the American Heart Association's *Life's Essential 8* program (Lloyd-Jones et al., 2022; Ma et al., 2023) that promotes pursuing and maintaining a healthy cardiovascular system with an overarching goal of increasing an individual's health span their lifespan, will be essential components of this strategy. Additionally, addressing upstream drivers of healthcare utilization including the determinants of health will be critical for reducing health disparities and ensuring equitable access to care. Effective stewardship in this context means creating a healthcare delivery system that actively produces positive health, optimizes wellness, and improves well-being across all population groups.

Another significant aspect of the future of healthcare stewardship is the increasing need for international collaboration, coordination, and cooperation. Existential global health challenges, such as emerging infectious disease outbreaks and the effects of the Anthropocene climate change on health status, will require intensive efforts from countries and healthcare organizations worldwide to manage and even reverse these threats to human existence. Strengthening global health governance, enhancing data sharing, analytics, and interoperability, and fostering cross-border partnerships will be essential for addressing these issues effectively. Furthermore, the development and implementation of robust healthy public policies that are adaptable to diverse contexts will help ensure that healthcare delivery systems can respond swiftly and efficient. By fostering cultural humility and shared responsibility, the global community can work together to build resilient healthcare delivery systems capable of withstanding these and any other future challenges (e.g., economic inequities and institutional bias and racism).

Finally, the moral and ethical dimensions of healthcare stewardship will continue to play a pivotal role in shaping the future of healthcare delivery world-wide. As new technologies and treatments emerge, moral and ethical considerations surrounding resource allocation, patient autonomy, and data access and privacy will become increasingly complex. Ensuring that healthcare decisions are made transparently and inclusively, with input from diverse healthcare stakeholders, will be critical for preserving public trust and achieving equitable health outcomes. Additionally, fostering a culture of continuous learning and improvement within healthcare organizations will be essential for adapting to changing circumstances and advancing the goals of healthcare stewardship. By prioritizing moral and ethical principles and embracing creativity and innovation, healthcare delivery systems can navigate the challenges that are sure to come in the not-so-distant future.

11.2 APPLYING HEALTHCARE STEWARDSHIP TO ACHIEVE BEST PRACTICE AND SUCCESSFUL OUTCOMES

To achieve best practices and successful health outcomes in healthcare stewardship, it is essential to implement a variety of empirically-supported and evidence-based strategies. These practices ensure the efficient, equitable, and effective use of healthcare resources. Below are examples of the key approaches discussed throughout this book to achieve healthcare stewardship.

1. Evidence-Based Medical Practices

    a. Clinical Practice Guidelines: Designing and implementing empirically-supported, evidence-based clinical practice guidelines is crucial for standardizing clinical care and reducing variability across healthcare delivery settings. These guidelines ensure that all patients receive high-quality, cost-effective interventions by providing clear, research-backed recommendations for treatment and management. By enhancing reliability and consistency in care, these guidelines help improve patient outcomes and optimize resource use, ultimately leading to a more effective and efficient healthcare system.

b. Continuous Learning: Encouraging continuous and comprehensive professional development and training for all clinical providers and staff is essential to keep pace with the latest evidence-based practices. By adopting the principles and practices of a learning health system, healthcare organizations can ensure that their workforce remains current with advancements in medical knowledge and technology. This ongoing education helps providers deliver the highest quality of care, fosters a culture of continuous improvement, and enhances overall patient outcomes by integrating the most recent and effective practices into everyday care focusing on healthcare stewardship principles.

c. Research and Innovation: Investing in, designing, and implementing empirically-supported healthcare research and development is crucial for advancing health outcomes. By leveraging advanced and innovative science and technologies, healthcare organizations can develop new treatments, diagnostic tools, and proactive measures that address current challenges and improve patient care. This commitment to research ensures that medical practices are based on the latest evidence and technologies, leading to more effective interventions, enhanced overall health outcomes, and healthcare stewardship.

2. Holistic, Integrated, Comprehensive and Coordinated Clinical Care

a. Holistic, Integrated, and Comprehensive Care: An interdisciplinary healthcare team, encompassing traditional medical services, essential public health services, and community-based organizations, collaborates to provide comprehensive care for individuals and the broader community. By employing a health equity and culturally competent approach, the team addresses the physical, psychological, and social aspects of health, striving to achieve positive health outcomes, optimize wellness, and enhance overall well-being. This integrated approach ensures that care is tailored to the diverse needs of patients, fostering a more inclusive and effective healthcare system while simultaneously monitoring for appropriate use of healthcare resources.

b. Care Coordination: Developing and implementing care coordination frameworks is essential to ensure that all patients, especially those with chronic conditions, have access to and receive the necessary navigation assistance during transitions of care across different healthcare settings. These frameworks facilitate smooth handoffs between providers, enhance communication, and streamline processes, ensuring continuity of care. By providing structured support and guidance, care coordination frameworks help patients manage their conditions more effectively, reduce gaps in care, and improve overall health outcomes.

c. Multidisciplinary Teams: Employing multidisciplinary teams to deliver evidence-based, value-added healthcare services ensures that care is both comprehensive and responsive to diverse patient needs. By integrating cultural humility and empathy into their approach, these teams address health disparities and work to close gaps in clinical care. This collaborative model emphasizes healthcare stewardship through enhancing the effectiveness of interventions and promoting equitable, people-centered care across various healthcare settings.

d. People-Centered Medical Homes: The people-centered medical home (PCMH) model of care is founded on principles and practices that include a whole-person orientation and team-based care. It emphasizes respect for patient preferences, needs, and values, delivered with cultural humility and empathy. The PCMH integrates healthcare services and functions, ensures seamless transitions of care, enhances access and navigation to care, and fosters open, bidirectional communication channels. It provides evidence-based services, engages in continuous quality improvement, empowers patients through self-management, addresses all determinants of health, and operates within a learning health system framework.

3. Health Information Technology

   a. Electronic Health Records (EHRs): Leveraging electronic health records (EHRs) enhances the accuracy, accessibility, and efficiency of both clinical and non-clinical patient information. This technology streamlines the management of secure data, facilitating better coordination and continuity of care during transitions within the healthcare system. By providing a comprehensive and up-to-date view of patient information, EHRs improve communication among providers and support seamless care delivery across different healthcare settings reducing wasteful and duplicative clinical care.

   b. Telemedicine: Expanding telemedicine can enhance access to care, especially in underserved and remote areas, and provide timely, convenient consultations for both physical and behavioral health issues. This growth requires improved broadband coverage and access to smart technology for the most vulnerable and marginalized patients.

   c. Data Analytics: Utilizing big data and data analytics allows healthcare organizations to identify trends, predict outcomes, and guide decision-making processes with greater precision. By analyzing vast amounts of data from diverse sources, such as patient records, clinical outcomes, and population health metrics, these tools uncover patterns and insights that inform targeted interventions and strategic planning. This approach enhances the ability to anticipate future health trends, optimize resource allocation, and improve patient care, ultimately leading to more effective and personalized healthcare solutions.

d. Interoperability: Improving the interoperability of health information systems and technology, along with expanding the use of Health Information Exchanges (HIEs), has become essential for a healthcare stewardship-influenced modern healthcare system. These advancements enable the seamless sharing of patient information across various healthcare providers and systems. Interoperability ensures that various electronic health records (EHR) systems can communicate and exchange data accurately, efficiently, and securely, regardless of the software used. HIEs act as centralized platforms or networks that enable the transfer of health information among diverse healthcare organizations, including hospitals, clinics, pharmacies, and public health agencies. This connectivity enhances the coordination of care, reduces the likelihood of medical errors, and improves clinical outcomes by providing healthcare professionals with timely and comprehensive access to patient records. By fostering a more integrated healthcare ecosystem, interoperability and HIEs also empower patients with better access to their health information, thereby promoting patient engagement and enabling more informed healthcare decisions.

e. Population Health Management (PHM) Platforms: Implementing a Population Health Management (PHM) platform serves as a comprehensive tool designed to improve health outcomes and optimize care for entire populations. These platforms integrate data from various sources, including electronic health records (EHRs), claims data, and patient surveys, to provide a holistic view of population health. By leveraging advanced analytics and data visualization, PHM platforms identify trends, assess risk factors, and stratify patient populations based on their health needs. This enables healthcare organizations to implement targeted interventions, manage chronic conditions more effectively, and promote preventive care. Additionally, PHM platforms facilitate care coordination among providers, streamline workflows, and support value-based care initiatives by monitoring performance metrics and patient outcomes. Ultimately, PHM platforms enhance the ability of healthcare systems to deliver personalized, efficient, and proactive care, improving overall population health and reducing healthcare costs.

4. Quality Improvement Initiatives

   a. Performance Measurement: Implementing performance measurement systems is essential for monitoring and evaluating the quality of care provided. By utilizing key performance indicators such as patient outcomes, readmission rates, emergency department (ED) volume, and patient satisfaction, healthcare organizations can assess the effectiveness of their services and identify areas for improvement. These measurements help ensure that care standards are met, facilitate continuous quality improvement, and ultimately lead to better patient outcomes and enhanced overall care delivery.

   b. Continuous Improvement: Fostering a culture of continuous improvement involves consistently evaluating and refining processes and practices to elevate the quality, safety, and efficiency of care provided. By routinely reviewing workflows, seeking feedback from staff and patients, and implementing data-driven changes, organizations can adapt to evolving needs, challenges, and efficiencies at scale.

This proactive approach not only enhances operational effectiveness but also ensures that care delivery remains people-centered and responsive. Embracing a mindset of ongoing refinement helps cultivate an environment where excellence is pursued relentlessly, benefiting both care providers and those they serve.

c. Accreditation and Certification: Pursuing accreditation and certification from nationally recognized organizations is essential for ensuring that healthcare facilities adhere to the highest standards of care. These prestigious endorsements validate that a facility meets rigorous criteria for quality, safety, and operational excellence. By engaging in this process, healthcare providers demonstrate their commitment to maintaining superior care practices, fostering trust with patients and stakeholders. Achieving and upholding these credentials not only enhances a facility's reputation but also drives continuous improvement, ultimately leading to better patient outcomes and more effective healthcare delivery.

5. Patient Engagement and Education

a. Shared Decision-Making: Involving patients in their own care decisions is crucial for ensuring they receive personalized and effective treatment. By providing patients with comprehensive information and supportive evidence-based resources, healthcare providers empower them to make informed choices about their health. This collaborative approach fosters greater engagement, enhances patient satisfaction and the patient experience, and leads to better adherence to treatment plans. When patients are actively involved in their care, they are more likely to feel respected and valued, which can significantly improve their overall health outcomes and experience with the healthcare system.

b. Health Literacy: Improving health literacy is essential for empowering patients to take control of their health by educating them about their conditions, treatment options, and proactive measures. By providing clear, accessible appropriate health information and using effective communication strategies, healthcare providers help patients understand their health preferences, needs, and values when making shared- informed decisions. This enhanced understanding not only supports better management of health conditions but also promotes engagement in proactive care. As patients become more knowledgeable about their health, they are better equipped to collaborate with their providers, leading to improved outcomes and a more effective healthcare experience.

c. Patient Feedback: Collecting and acting on patient feedback is vital for identifying areas for improvement and ensuring that care delivery aligns with patients' cultural needs, preferences, and values. By actively seeking and responding to patient input, healthcare providers can gain valuable insights into the effectiveness of their services and make necessary adjustments to better meet diverse patient needs. This approach fosters a more personalized and respectful care environment, enhances the patient experience, and builds trust and truthfulness between patients and providers. Addressing feedback in a thoughtful and responsive manner not only improves care quality but also helps create a more inclusive and responsive healthcare experience.

6. Resource Management

a. Cost-Effectiveness: Prioritizing cost-effective interventions ensures that healthcare resources are allocated in a way that maximizes health outcomes relative to their cost. By leveraging health technology assessments, healthcare providers can evaluate the effectiveness and economic impact of various interventions, guiding decisions toward those that offer the greatest benefit at the most reasonable cost. This approach not only helps in optimizing resource use but also supports the delivery of high-quality care within budgetary constraints. Implementing cost-effective strategies allows healthcare systems to enhance patient outcomes while maintaining financial sustainability.

b. Waste Reduction: Identifying and eliminating wasteful practices, such as unnecessary tests and procedures, is crucial for enhancing efficiency and reducing costs in healthcare. By scrutinizing and streamlining processes, healthcare providers can avoid redundant or non-beneficial activities that do not contribute to patient care, thereby optimizing resource use. This focus on minimizing waste not only helps in cutting costs but also improves overall care delivery by ensuring that resources are directed toward activities that offer real value. Streamlining practices leads to more efficient operations, better patient outcomes, and a more sustainable healthcare system.

c. Sustainable Practices: Implementing environmentally sustainable practices is essential for reducing the healthcare system's ecological footprint and promoting long-term sustainability. By adopting eco-friendly measures, such as reducing all forms of healthcare related-waste, conserving energy, and using sustainable materials, healthcare facilities can significantly lessen their environmental impact. These practices not only contribute to a healthier planet but also align with broader goals of sustainability, ultimately benefiting both current and future generations. Adopting green initiatives in healthcare promotes a holistic, integrated, and comprehensive stewardship approach to health, wellness, and well-being recognizing that individual, family, and community health is closely linked to environmental health.

d. Medical Supply Chain Management: Regular assessments of supply chain activity are crucial for identifying and addressing early bottlenecks in structures and processes. By systematically evaluating supply chain performance, healthcare organizations can pinpoint inefficiencies, delays, or obstacles before they escalate into more significant issues. This proactive approach enables timely interventions to streamline operations, improve workflow, and ensure the consistent availability of necessary resources. Effective supply chain management not only enhances overall efficiency but also supports uninterrupted patient care and optimal operational performance.

7. Health Equity and Access

a. Equitable Resource Allocation: Ensuring equitable distribution of healthcare resources is vital for reducing health disparities, particularly among underserved and vulnerable populations. By prioritizing these groups, healthcare systems can address gaps in access and care, providing essential services where they are most needed. This approach promotes fairness and helps to rectify systemic imbalances, ensuring that all individuals receive appropriate and timely care. Focusing on equitable resource allocation contributes to a more inclusive healthcare system, ultimately improving overall public health and reducing disparities.

b. Access and Navigation to Care: Improving access to evidence-based medical care requires implementing healthy public policies and programs that address barriers such as geographic location, socio-economic status, and cultural differences. By developing initiatives that specifically target these challenges, healthcare delivery systems can enhance navigation and ensure that quality care reaches all individuals, regardless of their circumstances. Healthy public policies that expand healthcare coverage, support telemedicine, and provide culturally competent care are essential for overcoming these barriers. This comprehensive approach promotes equitable access to healthcare, ultimately leading to better health outcomes and a more inclusive healthcare environment.

c. Community Health Initiatives: Developing and supporting community health initiatives that address all determinants of health requires close collaboration with community-based organizations and community-oriented primary care. By working together, these entities can create comprehensive strategies that tackle the social, economic, and environmental factors influencing health. Engaging with local communities ensures that initiatives are tailored to specific needs and conditions, fostering more effective and sustainable health solutions. This collaborative approach not only enhances the reach and impact of health programs but also empowers communities to actively participate in improving their own health, wellness, and well-being.

d. Community-based Organizations: Implementing closed-loop referrals for upstream, non-clinical determinates of health and fully engaging with cultural humility and empathy are crucial for providing comprehensive and effective care. For instance, programs like *Food as Medicine* and *Non-Emergent Medical Transportation (NEMT)* address specific patient needs beyond traditional clinical settings, ensuring that individuals receive comprehensive support. By approaching these services with cultural humility, healthcare providers acknowledge and respect diverse backgrounds, fostering trust and truthfulness and improving patient engagement. This empathetic and integrated approach helps bridge gaps in care, enhances patient outcomes, and supports overall health, wellness, and well-being by addressing both medical and social determinants of health.

8. Governance, Leadership, and Accountability

   a. Transparent Decision-Making: Ensuring that healthcare decisions are made transparently and involve input from a diverse array of stakeholders is essential for fostering trust and truthfulness and achieving balanced outcomes. By incorporating perspectives from patients, providers, and policymakers, healthcare delivery systems can address the needs and concerns of all parties involved, leading to more informed and equitable decisions. This inclusive approach not only enhances accountability and transparency but also promotes collaboration and shared responsibility in shaping effective healthcare policies and practices. Engaging all relevant stakeholders ensures that decisions reflect a comprehensive understanding of the challenges and opportunities within the healthcare system.

   b. Accountability Mechanisms: Implementing accountability mechanisms is crucial for ensuring that healthcare providers and organizations adhere to established best practices and standards of healthcare stewardship. By setting clear performance benchmarks and regularly monitoring adherence, these mechanisms hold providers accountable for their actions and outcomes. This includes conducting audits, implementing performance reviews, and establishing transparent reporting systems. Such measures not only promote consistent delivery of high-quality care but also foster a culture of continuous improvement, where providers are motivated to maintain and exceed established standards. Ensuring accountability helps enhance patient safety, optimize care quality, and build trust within the healthcare system.

   c. Policy and Regulation: Developing and enforcing policies and regulations that promote high standards of care, protect patient rights, and ensure the responsible use of healthcare resources is essential for maintaining a healthcare stewardship-centric healthcare delivery system. These policies provide clear guidelines and accountability, ensuring that care is delivered consistently and ethically while safeguarding patient health, safety, and welfare. Regulations that address healthcare resource allocation and management help to prevent waste and misuse, promoting efficient and effective care. By establishing and upholding these standards, healthcare systems can enhance patient safety, uphold ethical practices, and optimize the use of resources, ultimately leading to improved health outcomes and overall system integrity.

d. Trust and Truthfulness: Leadership that prioritizes factual and verifiable information fosters full engagement among all healthcare stakeholders by promoting transparency, trust, and integrity. When leaders base their decisions and communications on accurate data, they facilitate multi-directional communication, enabling open dialogue between providers, patients, policymakers, and other key parties. This evidence-based approach ensures that all stakeholders are informed and aligned, leading to more effective collaboration and decision-making. By upholding a commitment to factual accuracy, leaders can drive informed, constructive interactions and support a cohesive, responsive healthcare environment focused on the principles and practices of healthcare stewardship.

In summary, achieving best practice and successful outcomes in healthcare stewardship requires a multifaceted approach that integrates in a healthcare delivery system both horizontally and vertically focusing on evidence-based practices, coordinated care, advanced health information technology, continuous quality improvement, population health management, patient engagement, efficient resource management, health equity, and robust governance. By focusing on these foundational areas, healthcare systems can enhance the quality, efficiency, and equity of care, ultimately leading to better health outcomes for both individuals and the community-at large.

11.3 REFERENCES

Lloyd-Jones, D. M., Ning, H., Labarthe, D., et al. (2022) Status of cardiovascular health in US adults and children using the American Heart Association's new "Life's Essential 8" metrics: prevalence estimates from the National Health and Nutrition Examination Survey (NHANES), 2013 through 2018. *Circulation*146 (11): 822-835.

Ma, H., Wang, X., Xue, Q., et al. (2023) Cardiovascular health and life expectancy among adults in the United States.*Circulation* 147 (15): 1137-1146.

Maleki-Varnosfaderani, S., Forouzanfar, M. (2024) The role of AI in hospitals and clinics: transforming healthcare in the 21st century.*Bioengineering* 11 (4): 337.

www.ingramcontent.com/pod-product-compliance
Lightning Source LLC
Chambersburg PA
CBHW062129020426
42335CB00013B/1154